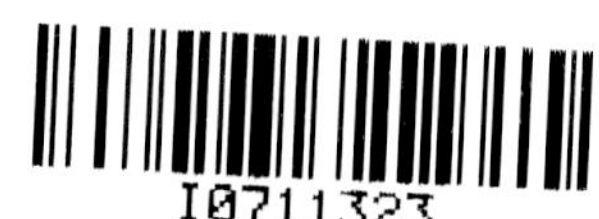

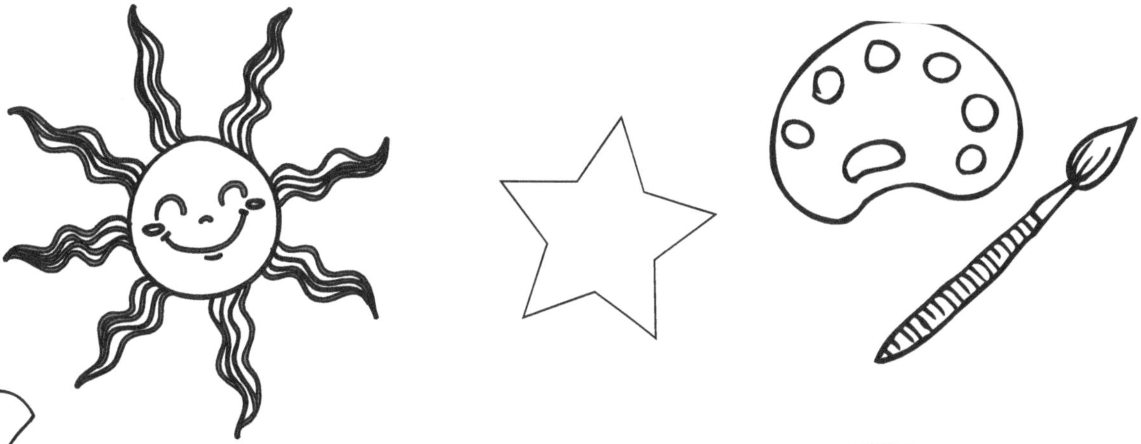

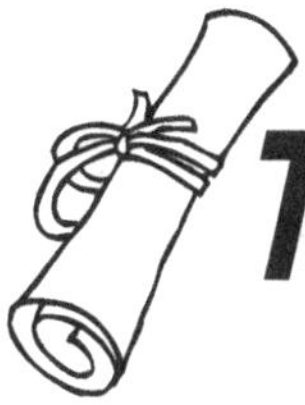

This Book Belongs To

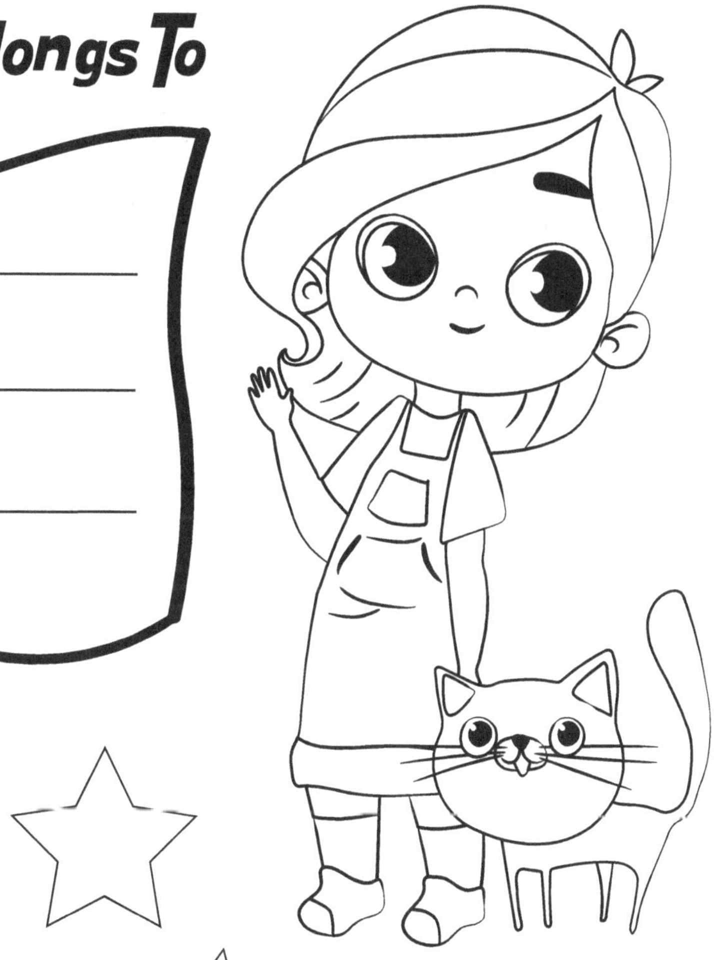

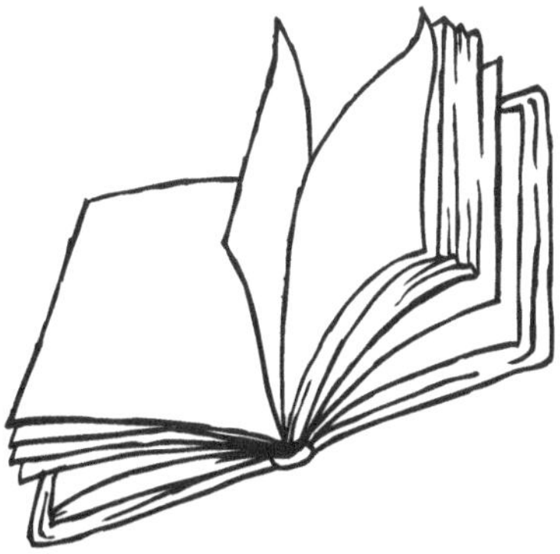

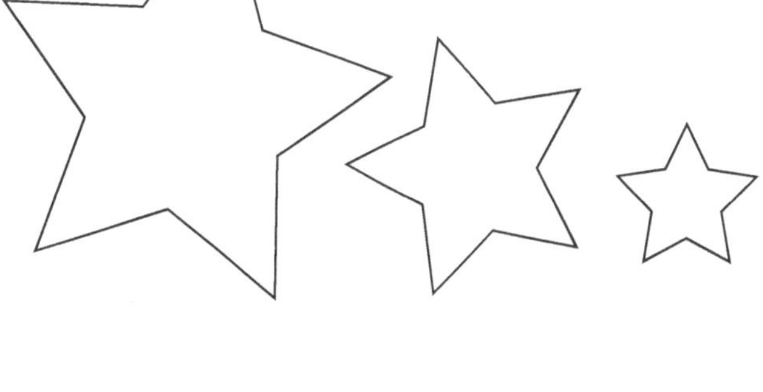

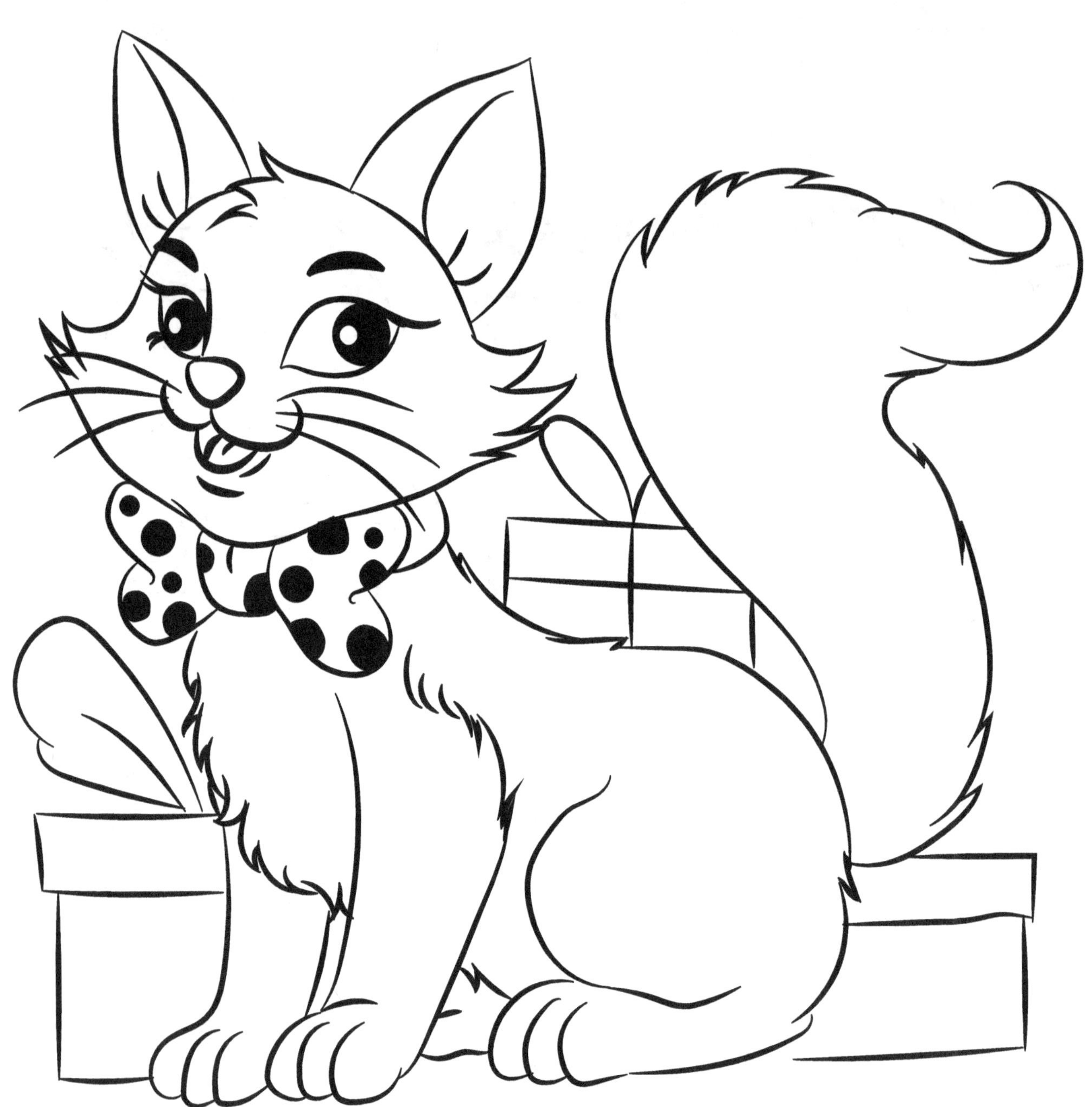

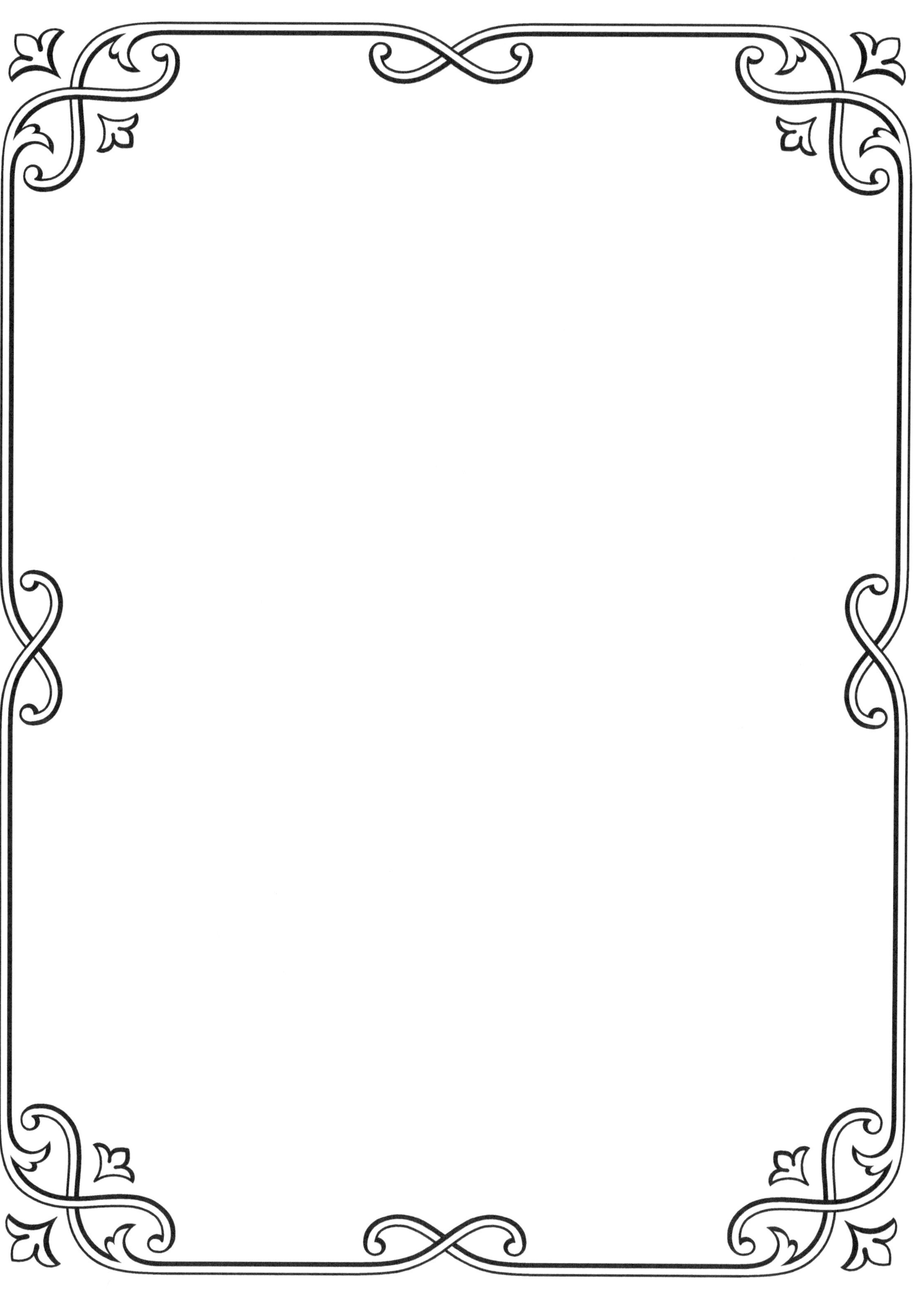

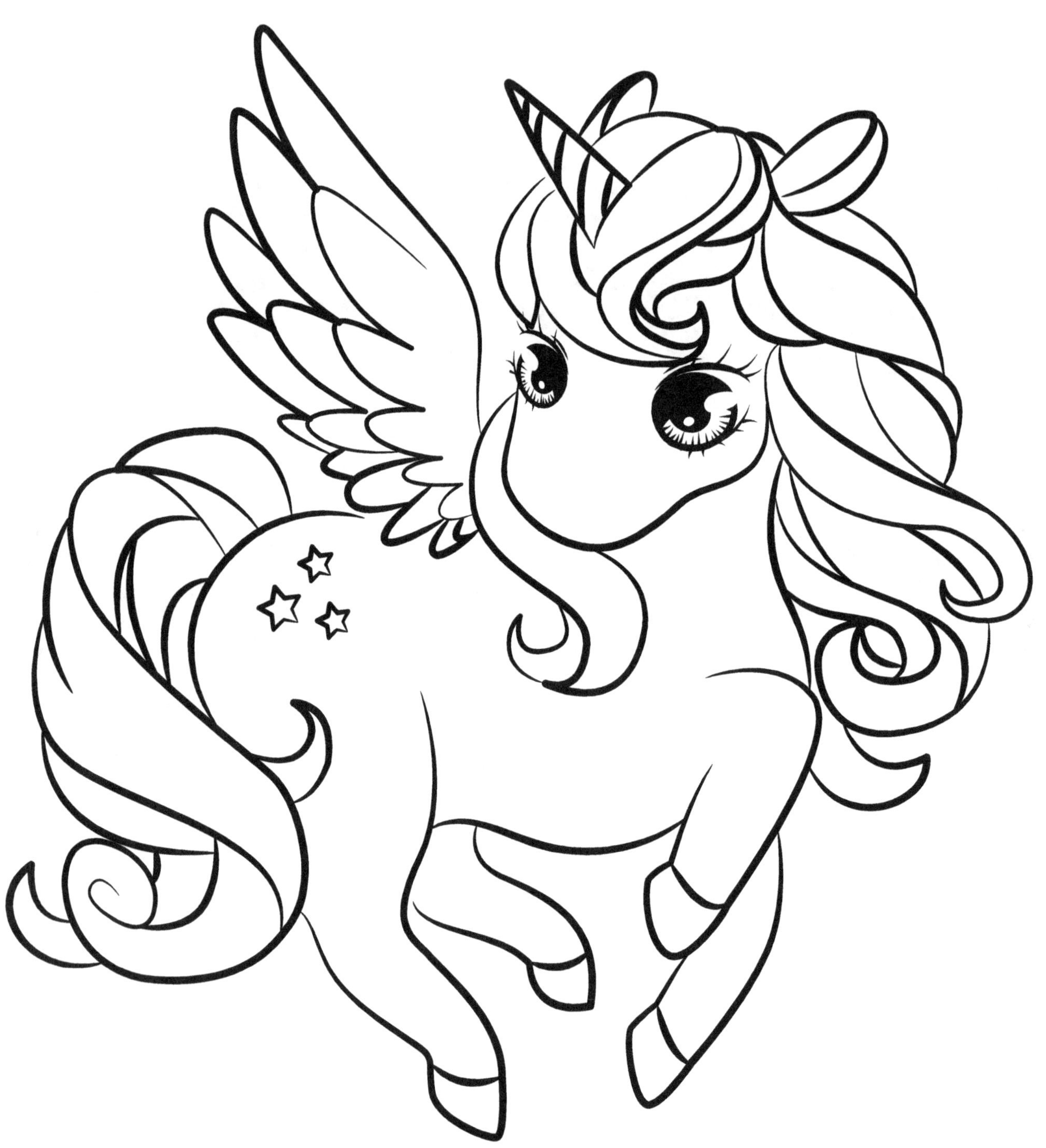

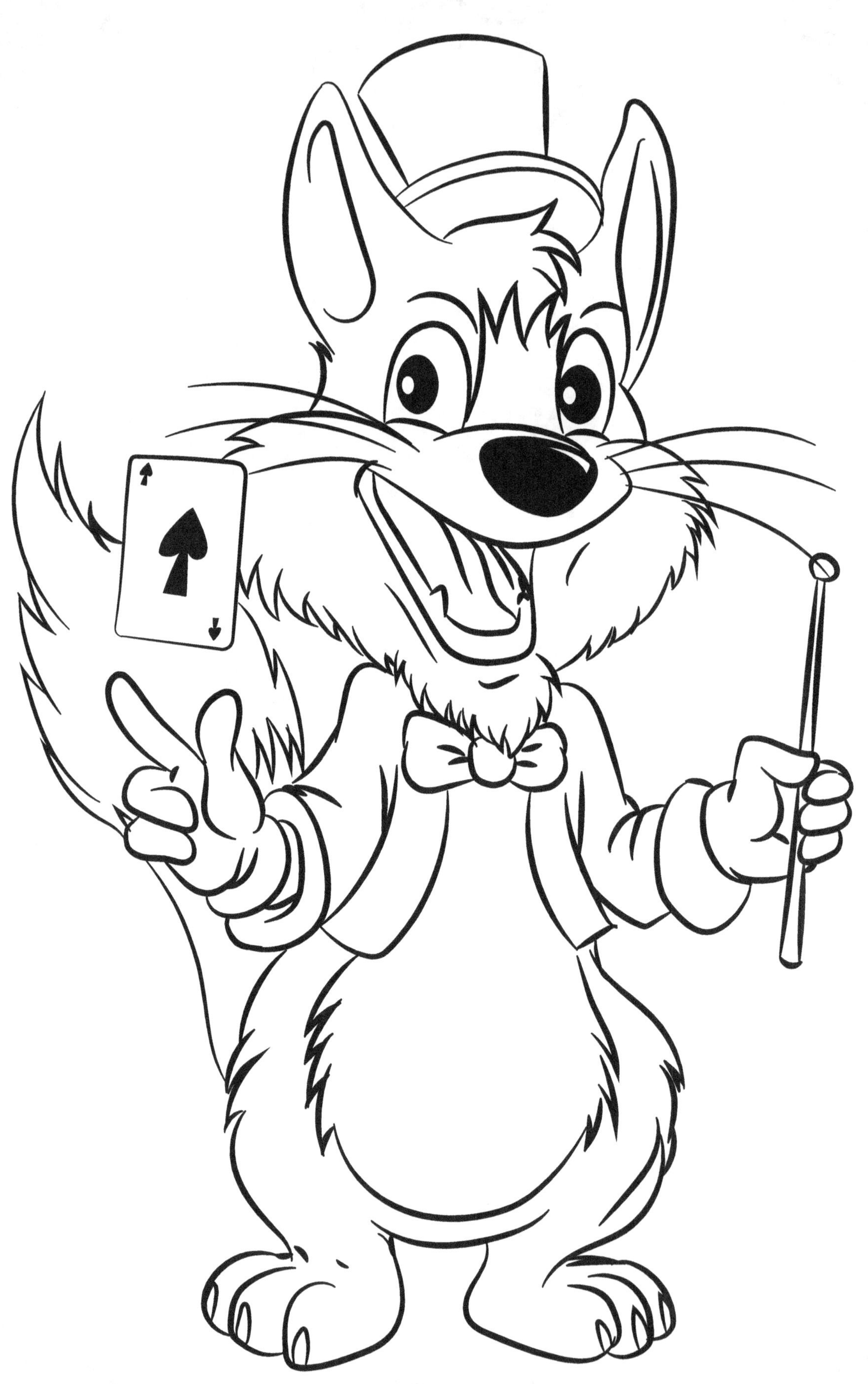

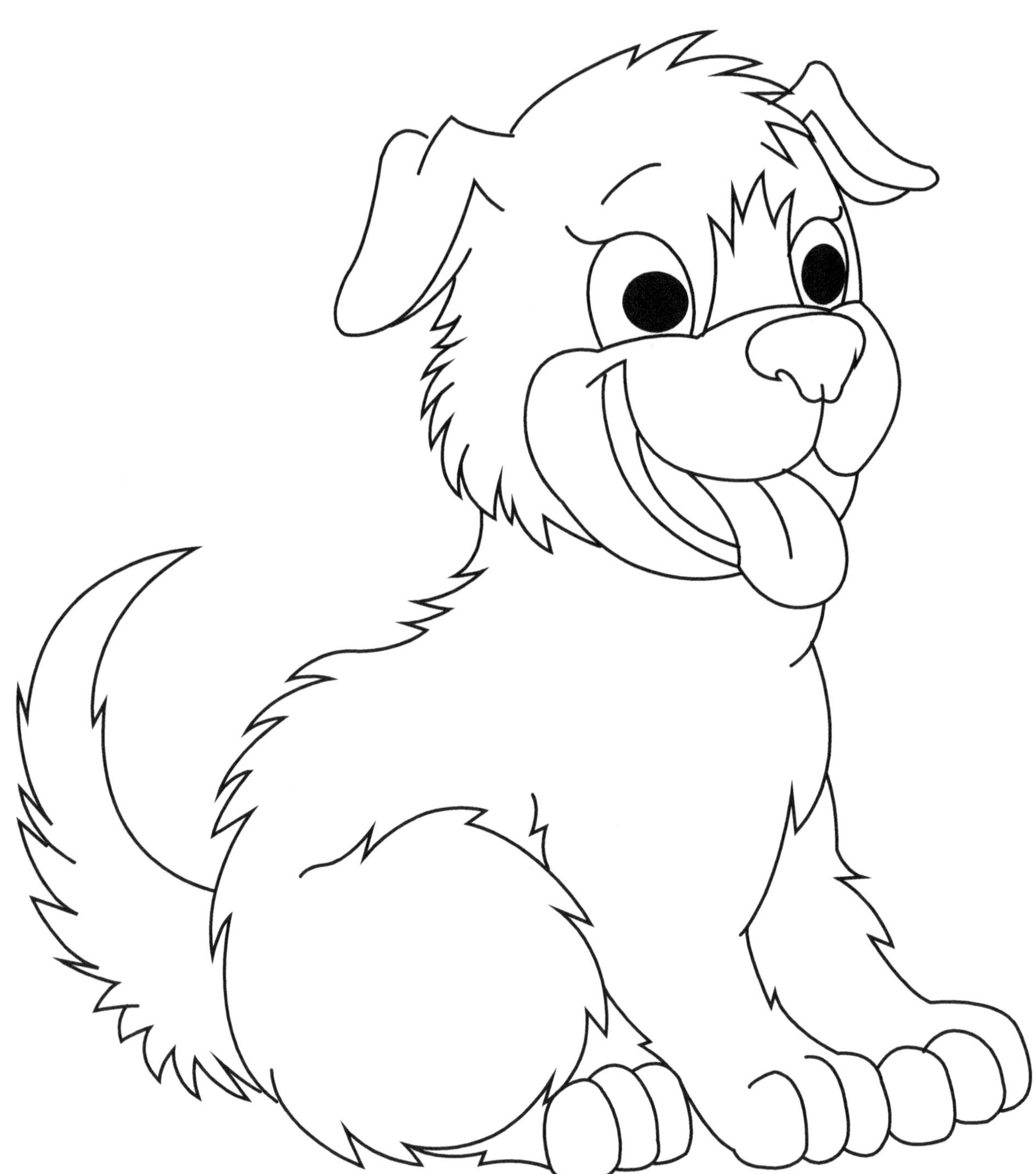

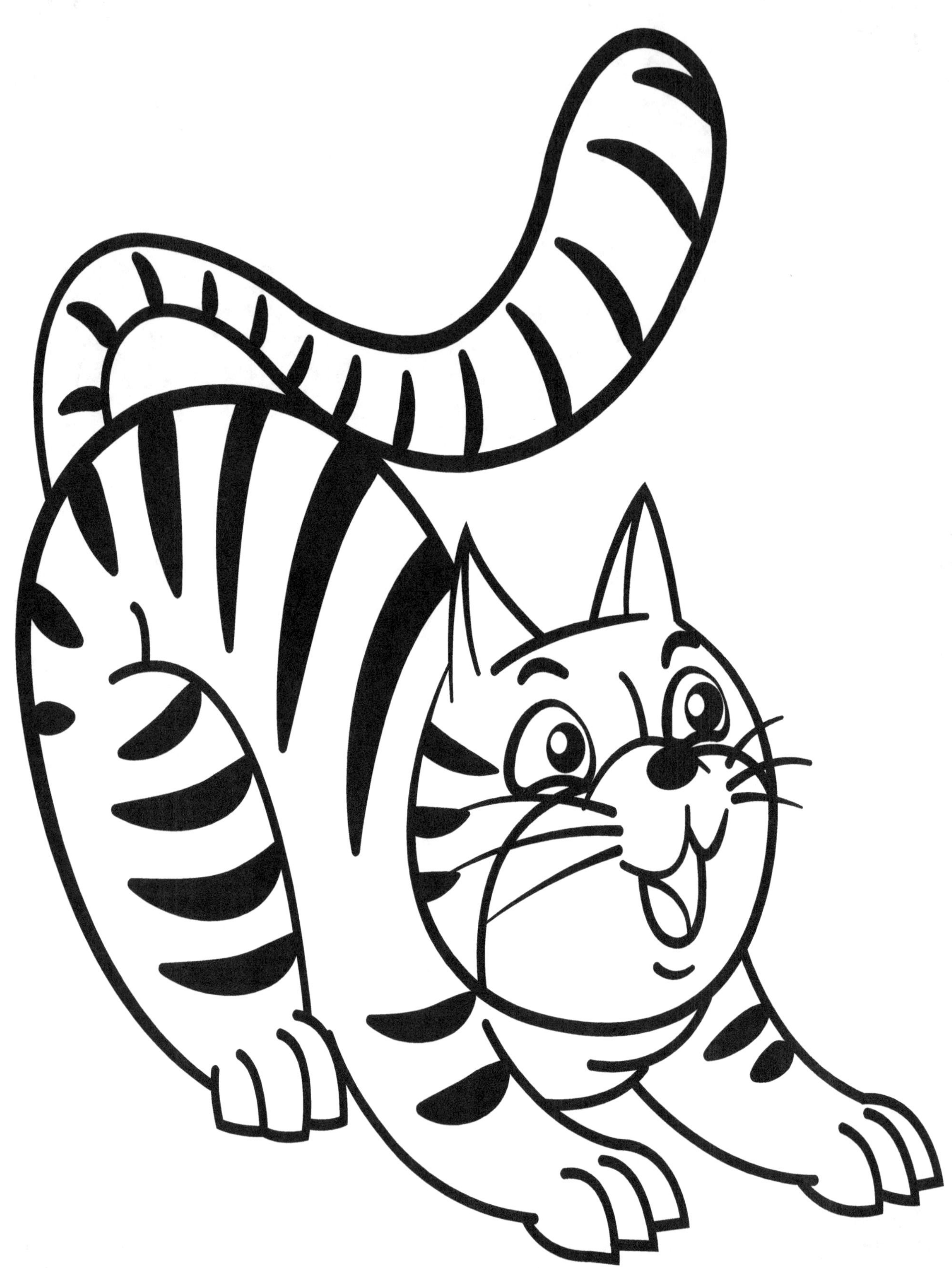

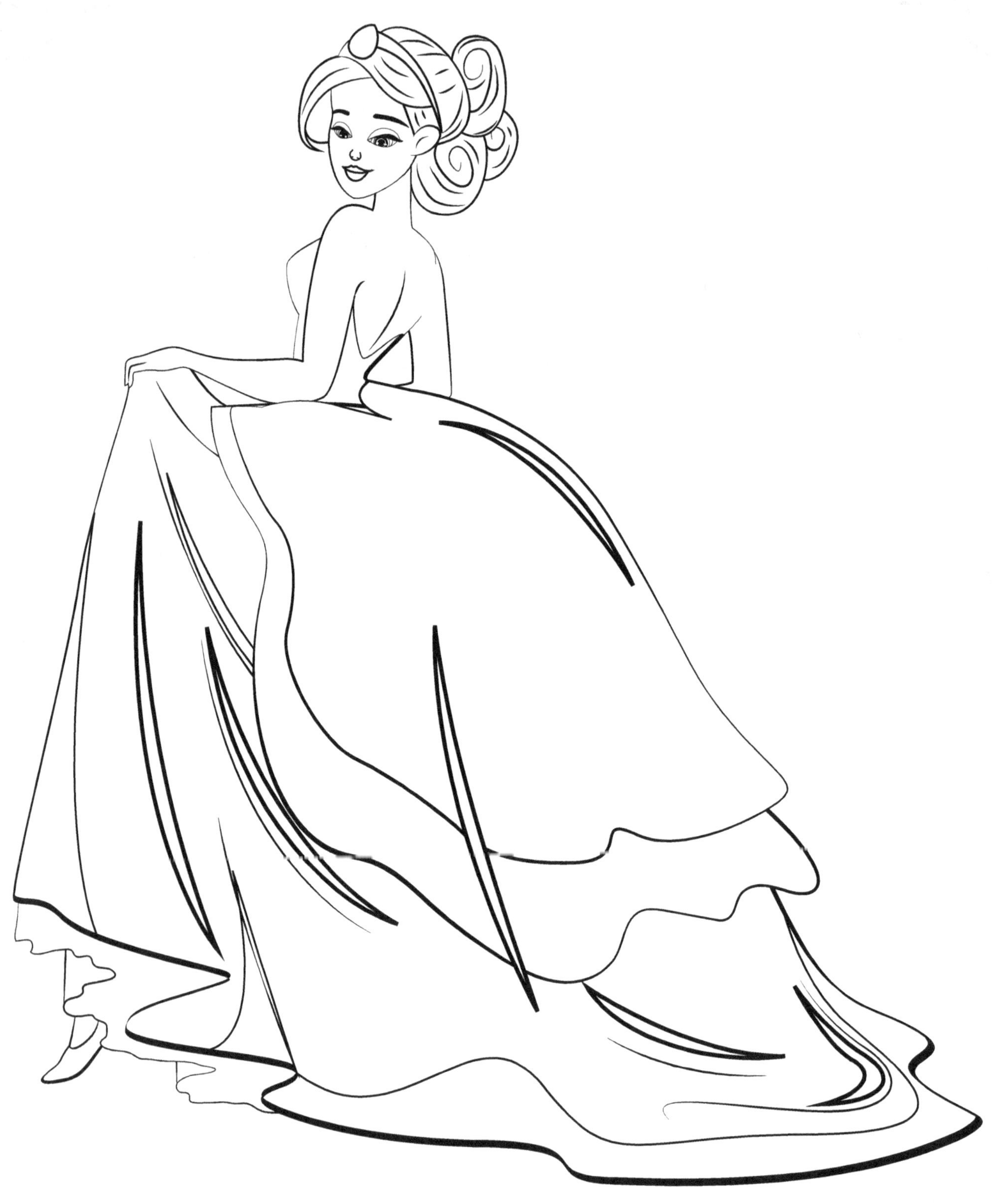

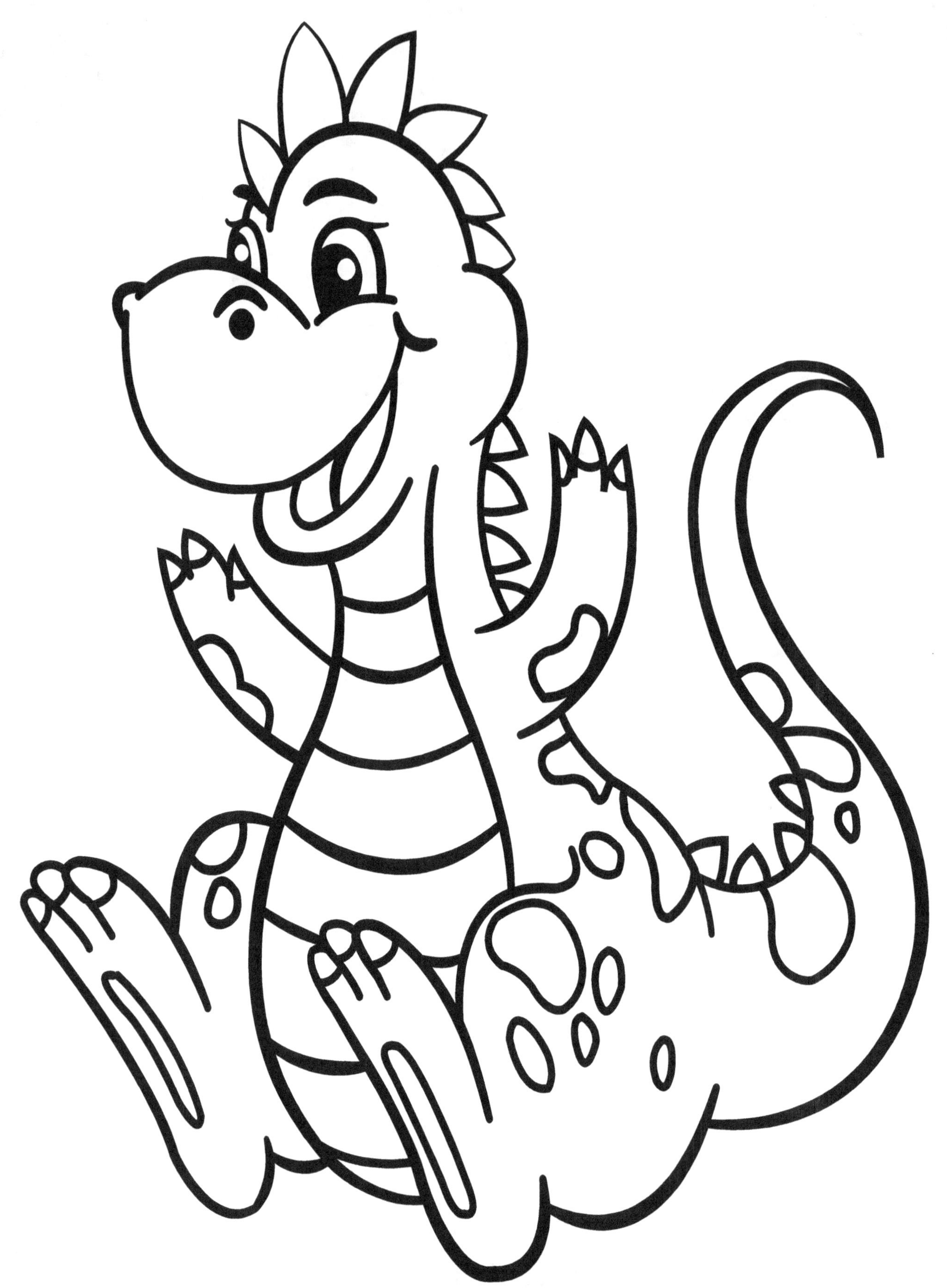

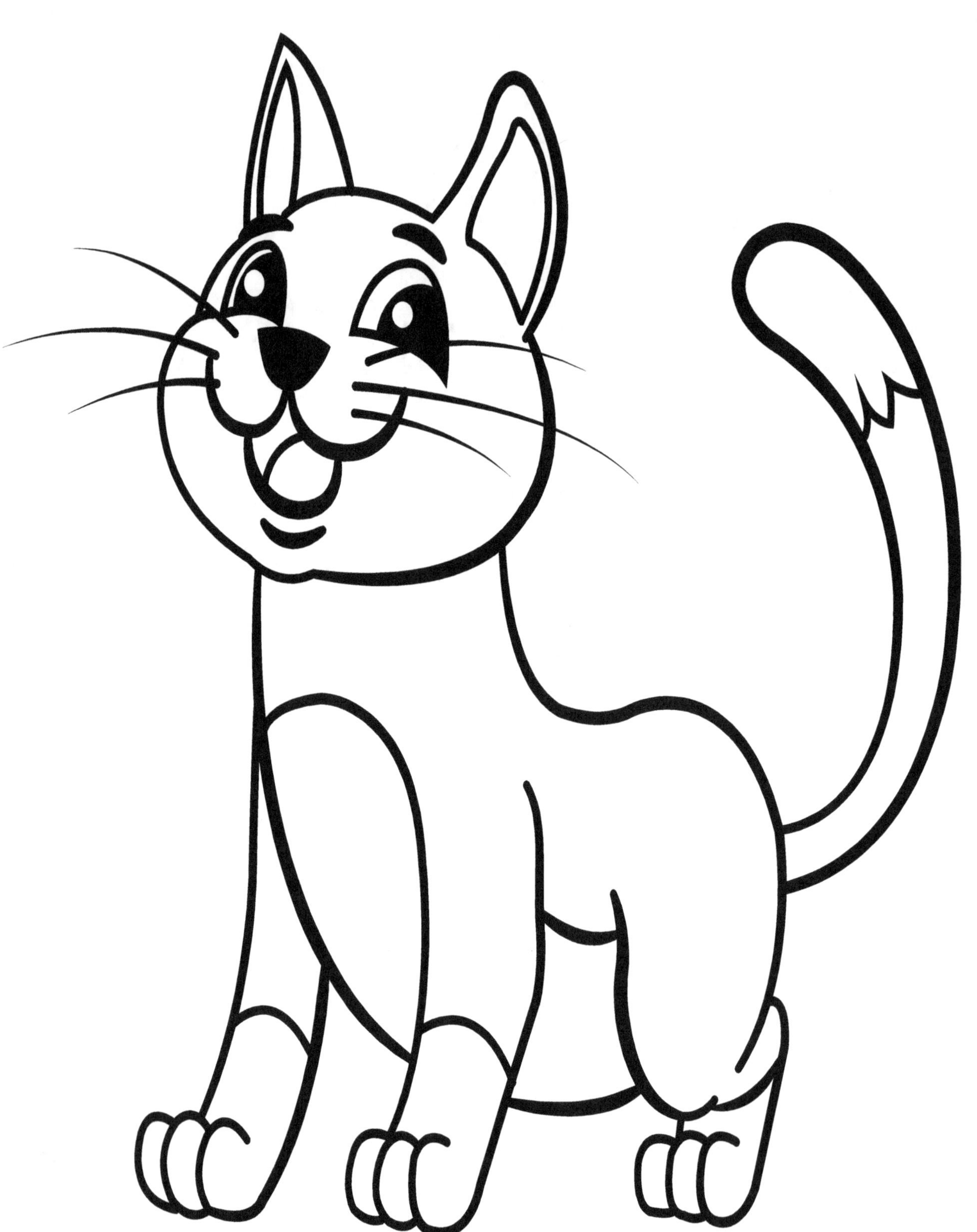

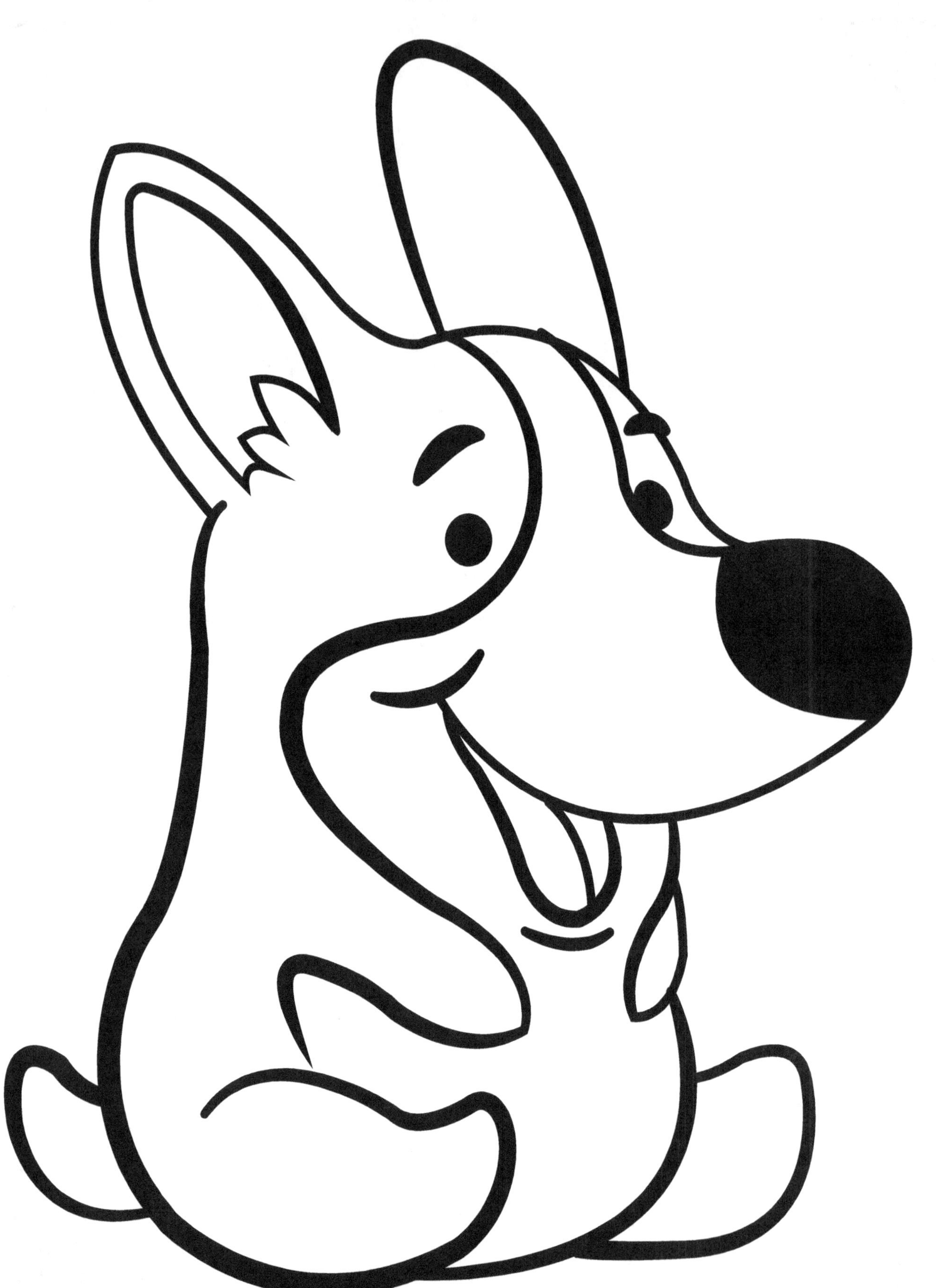

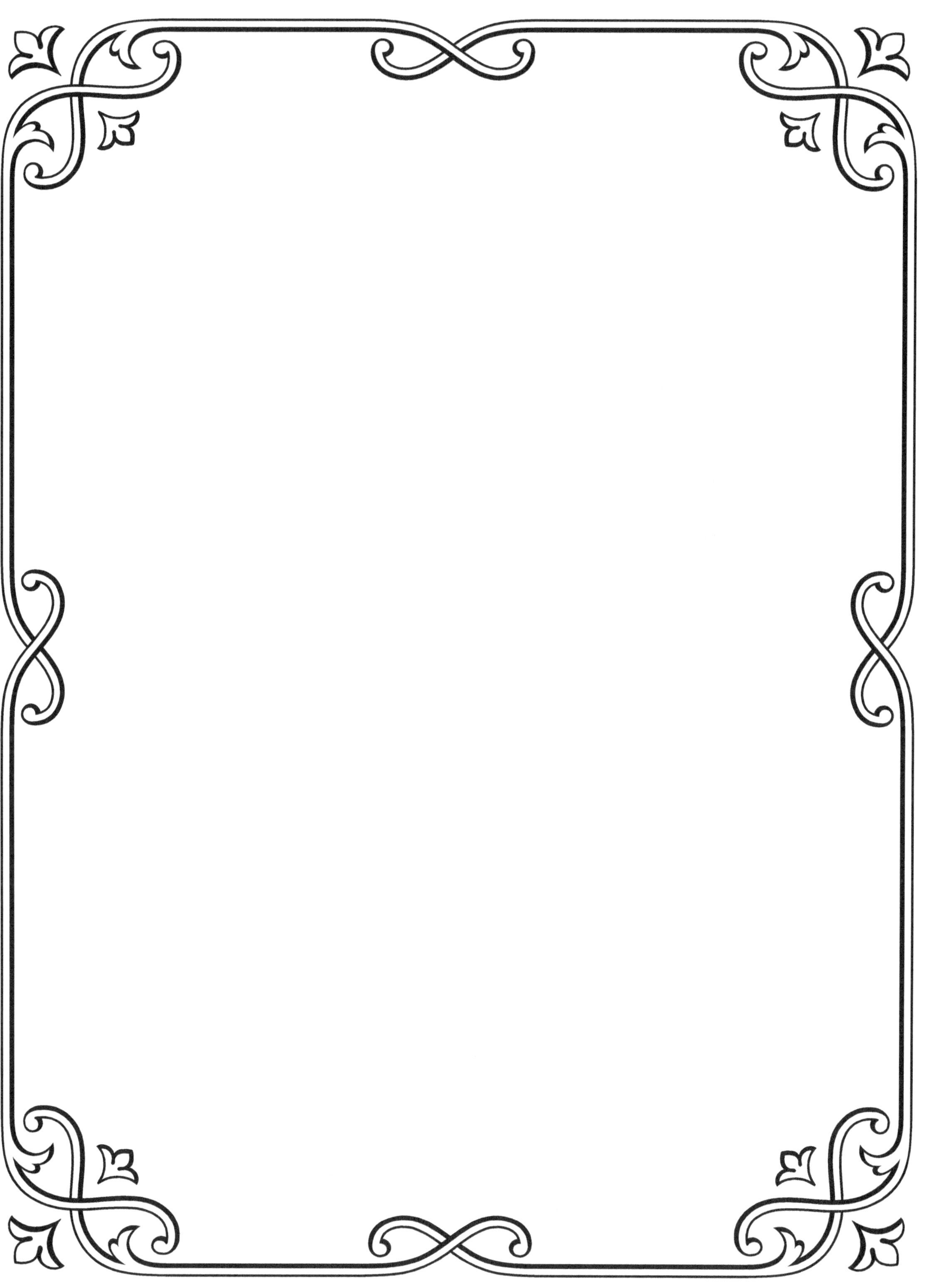

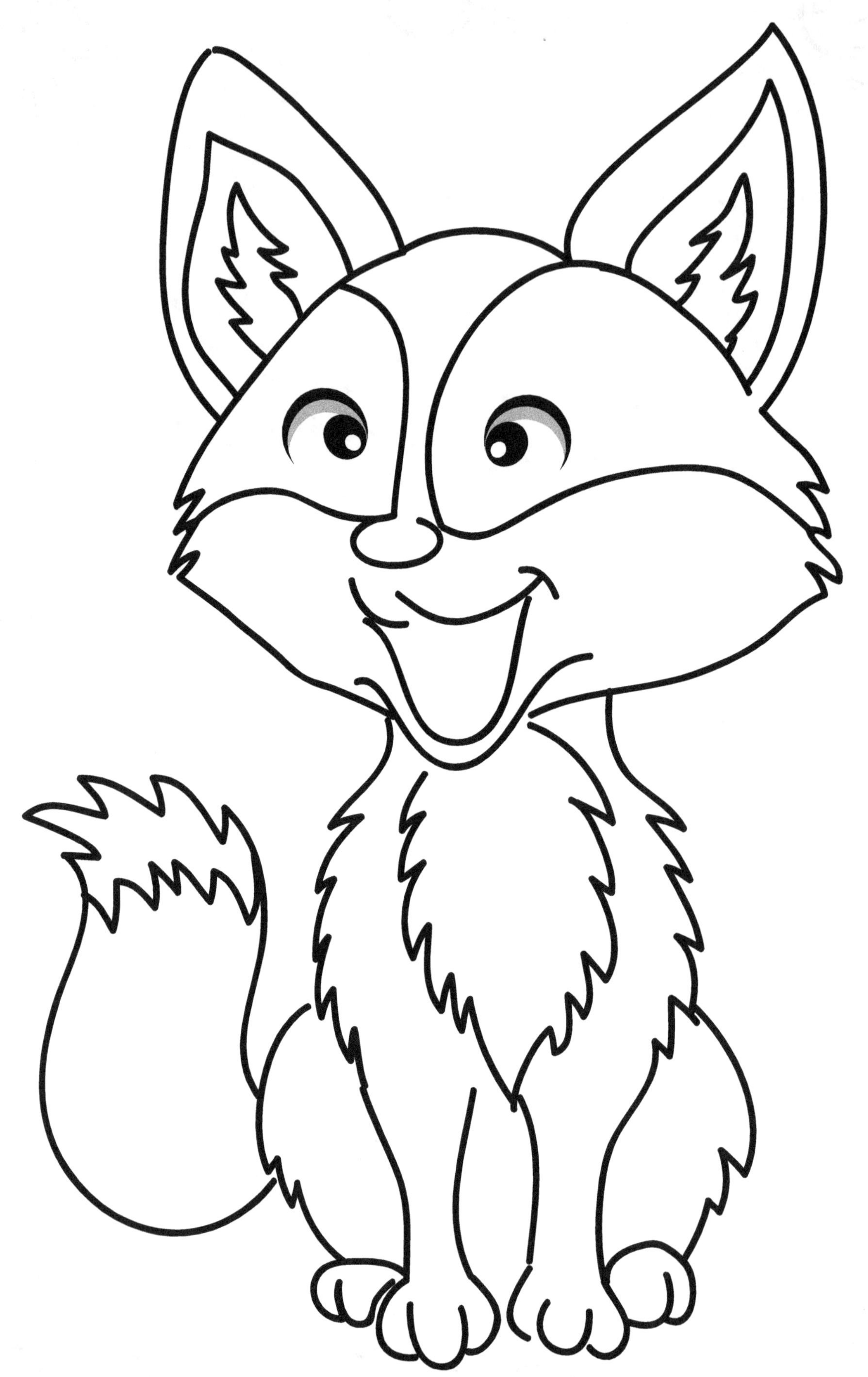

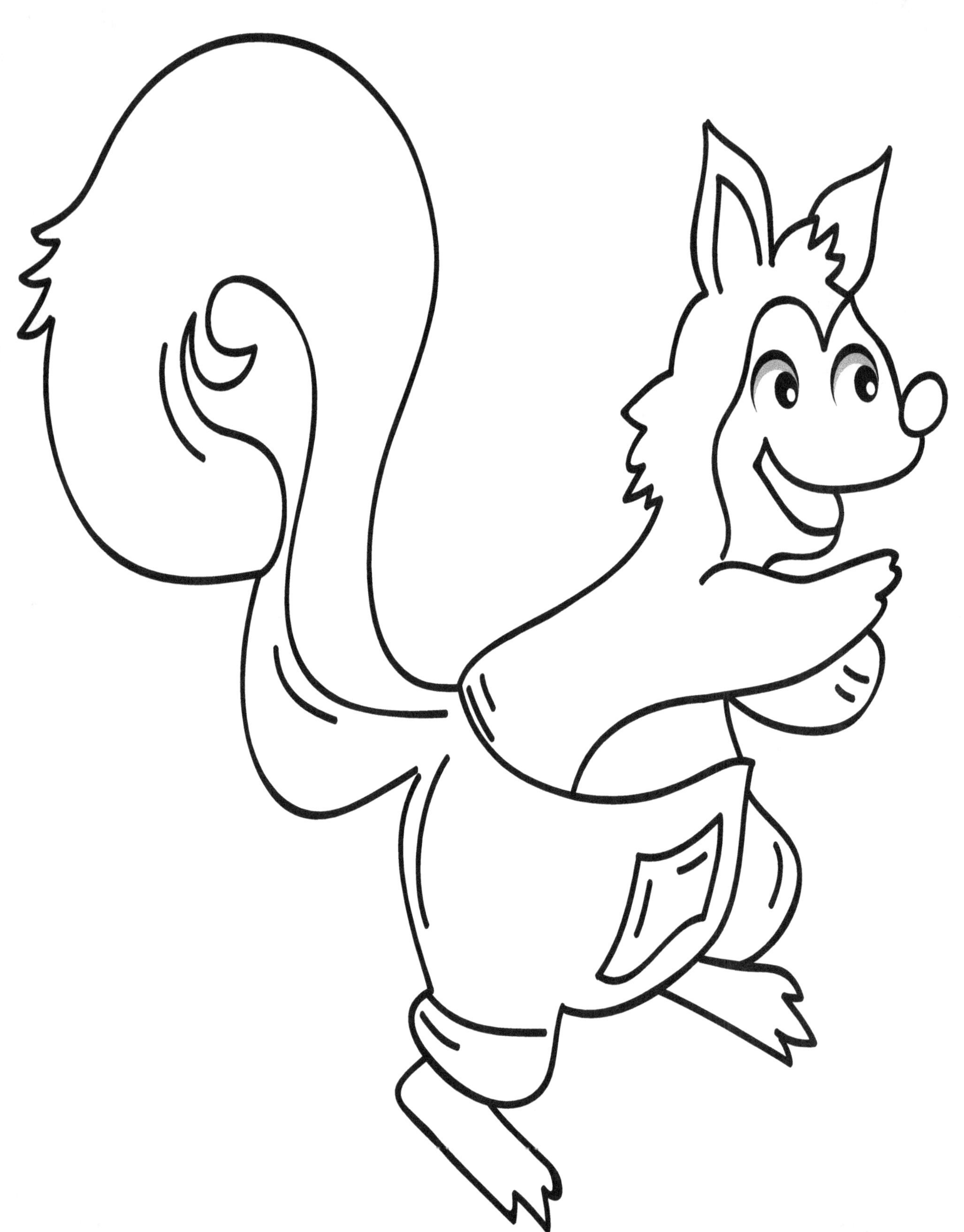

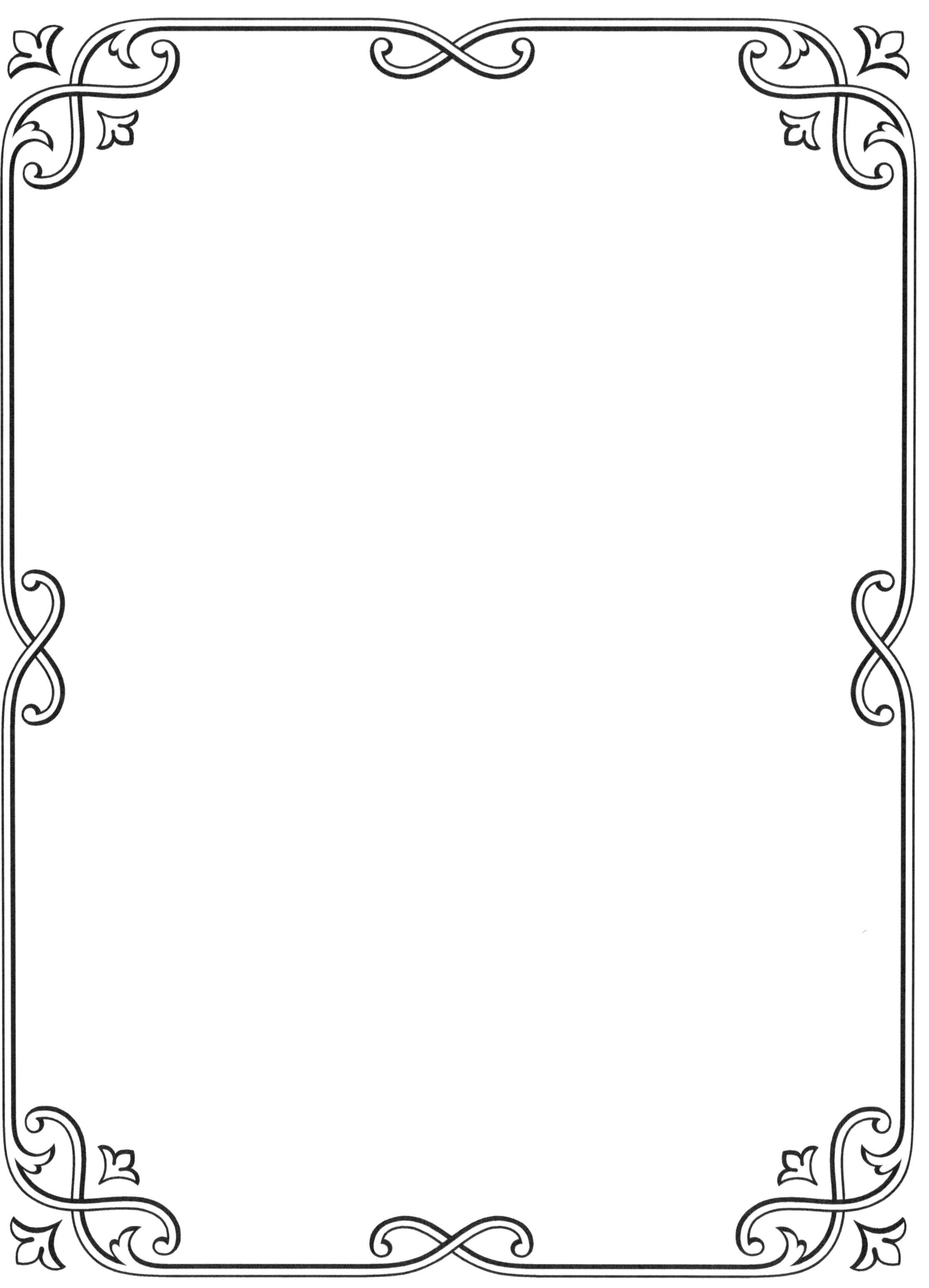

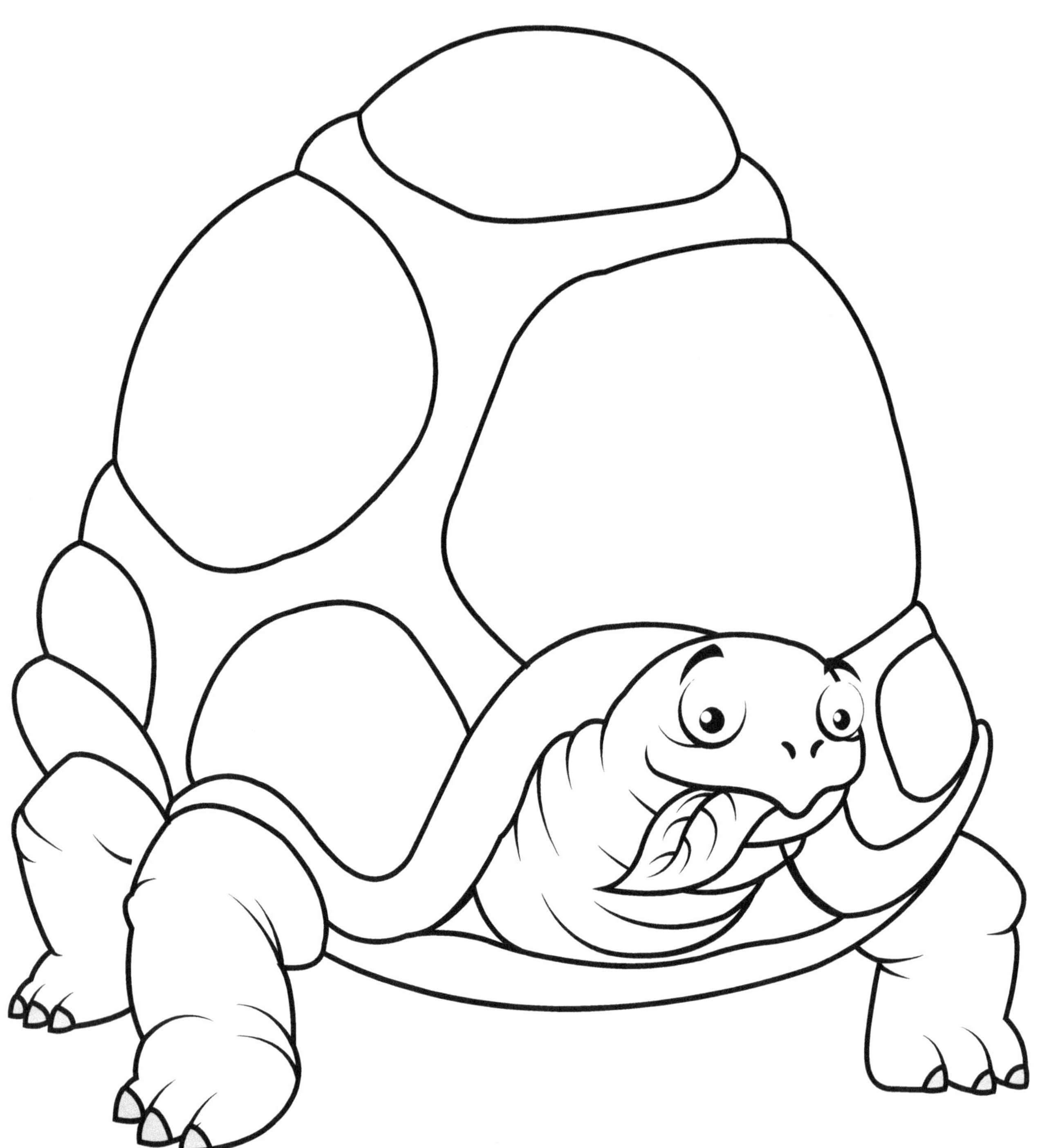

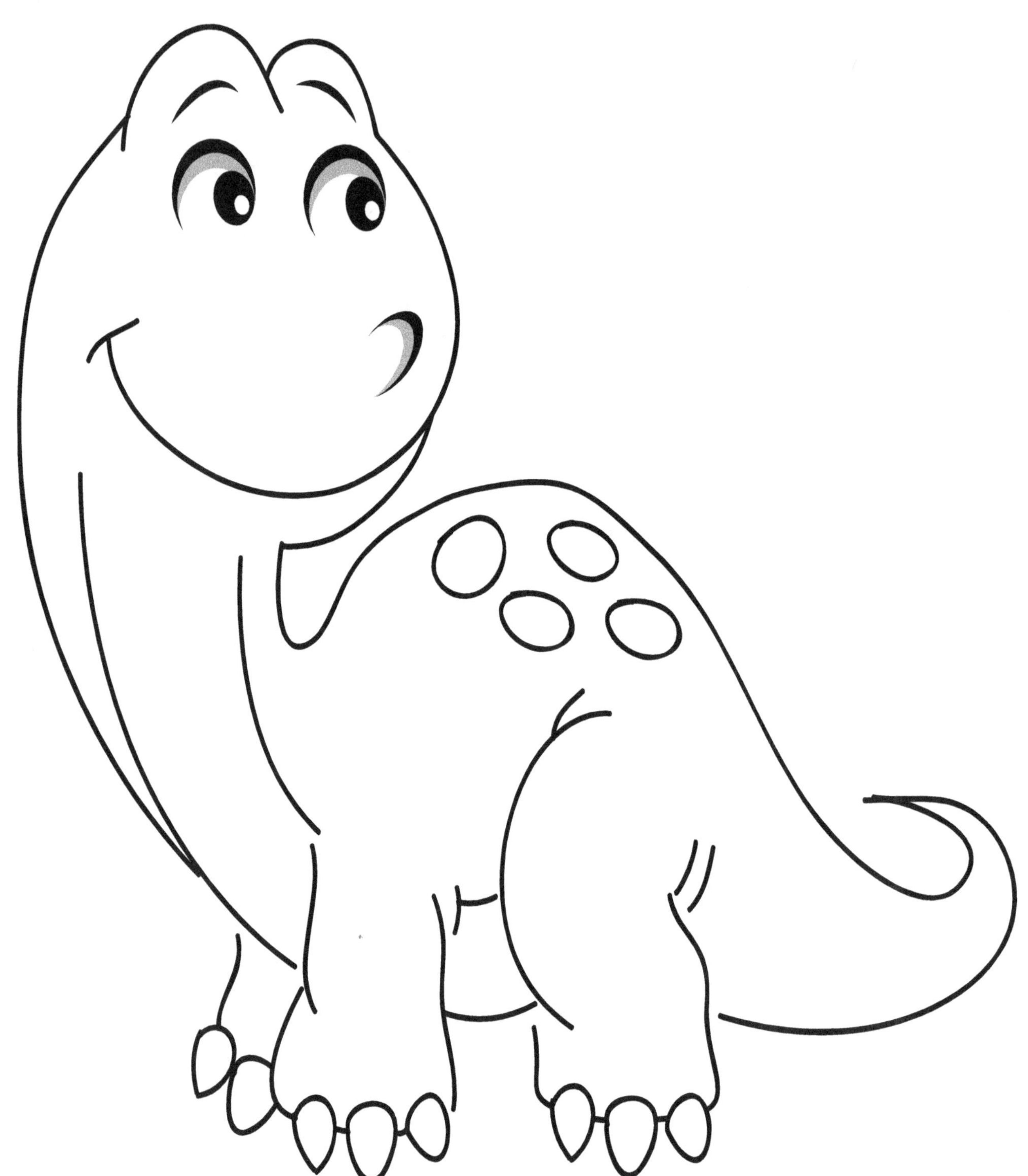

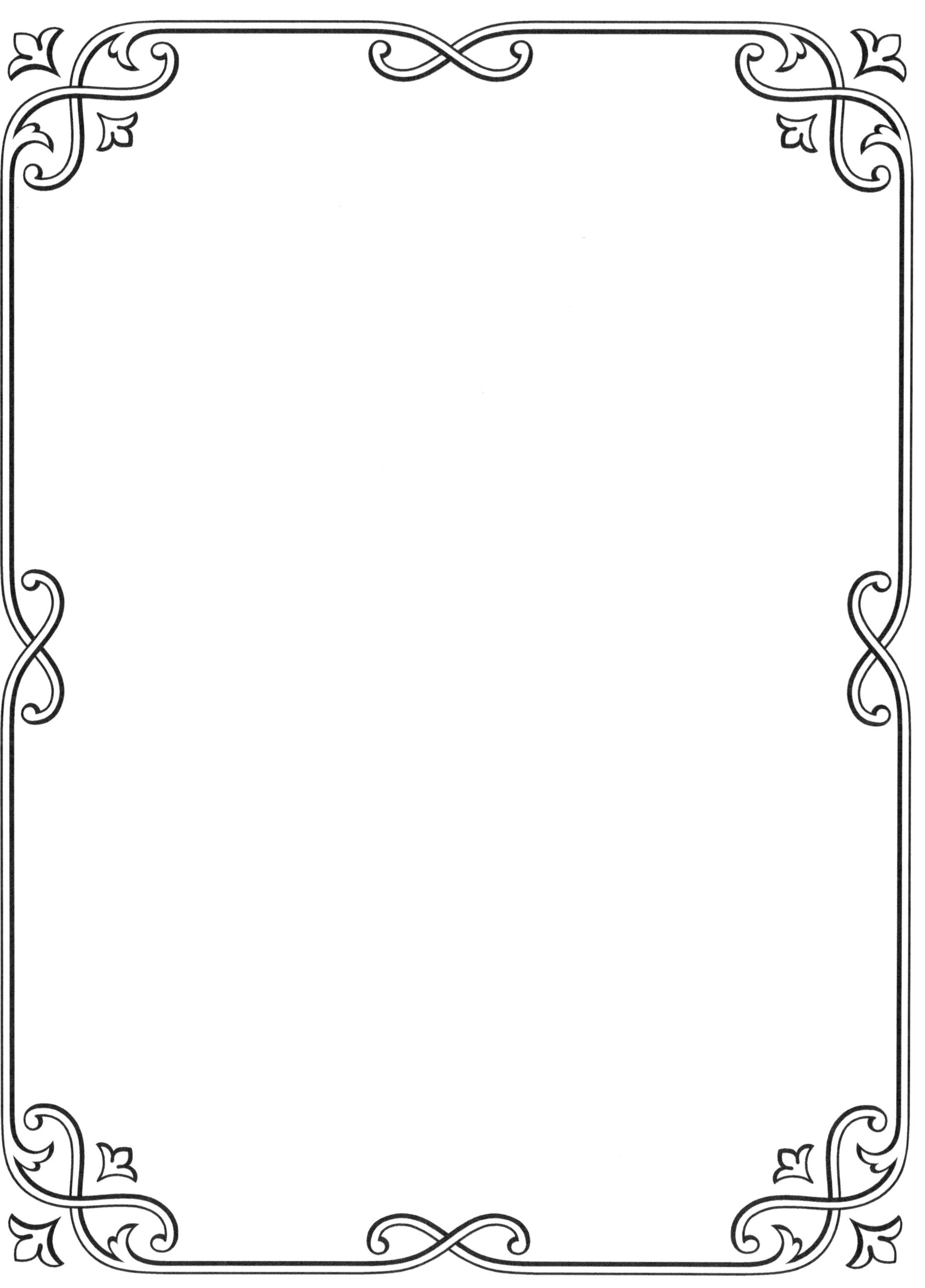

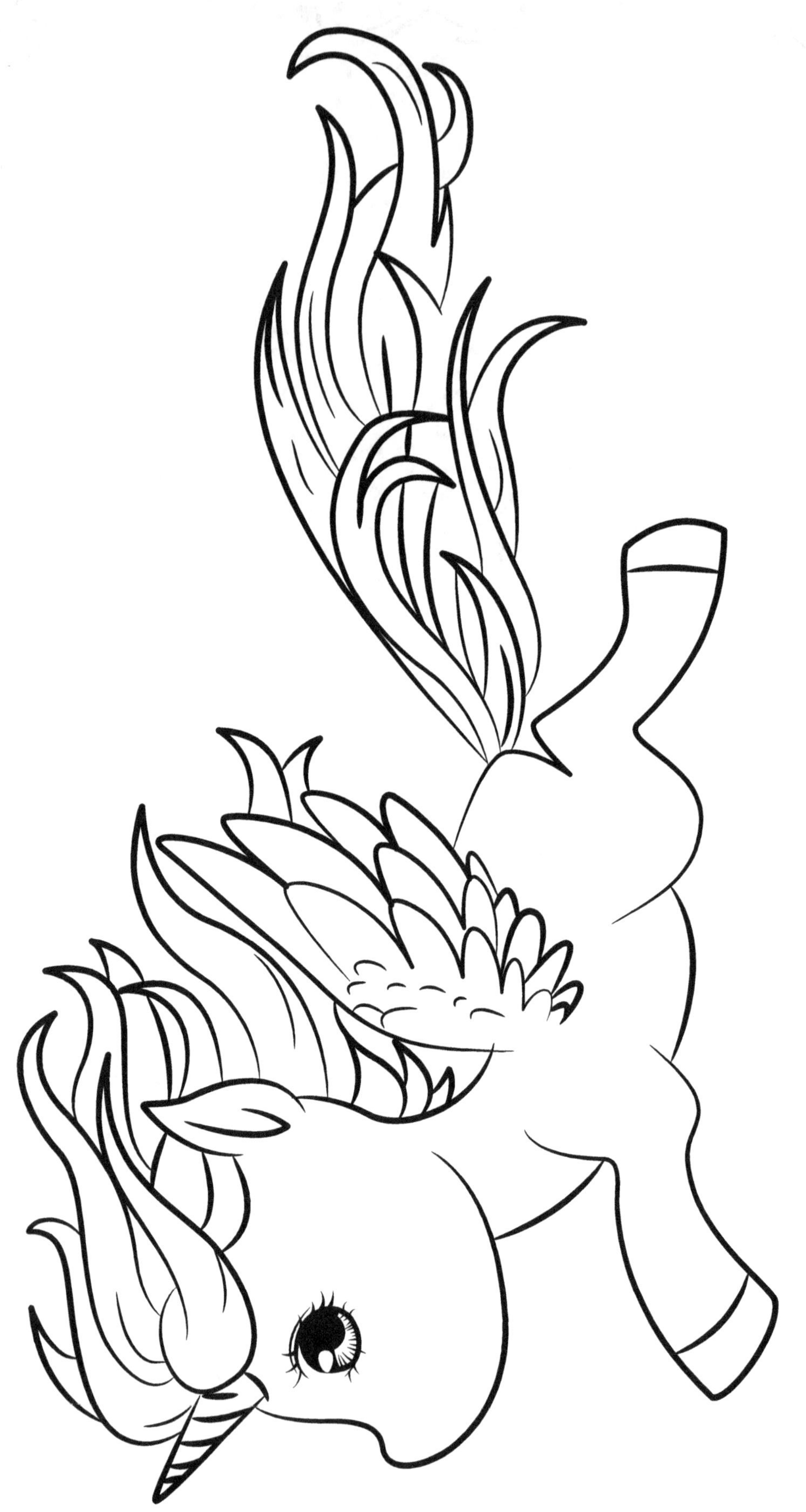

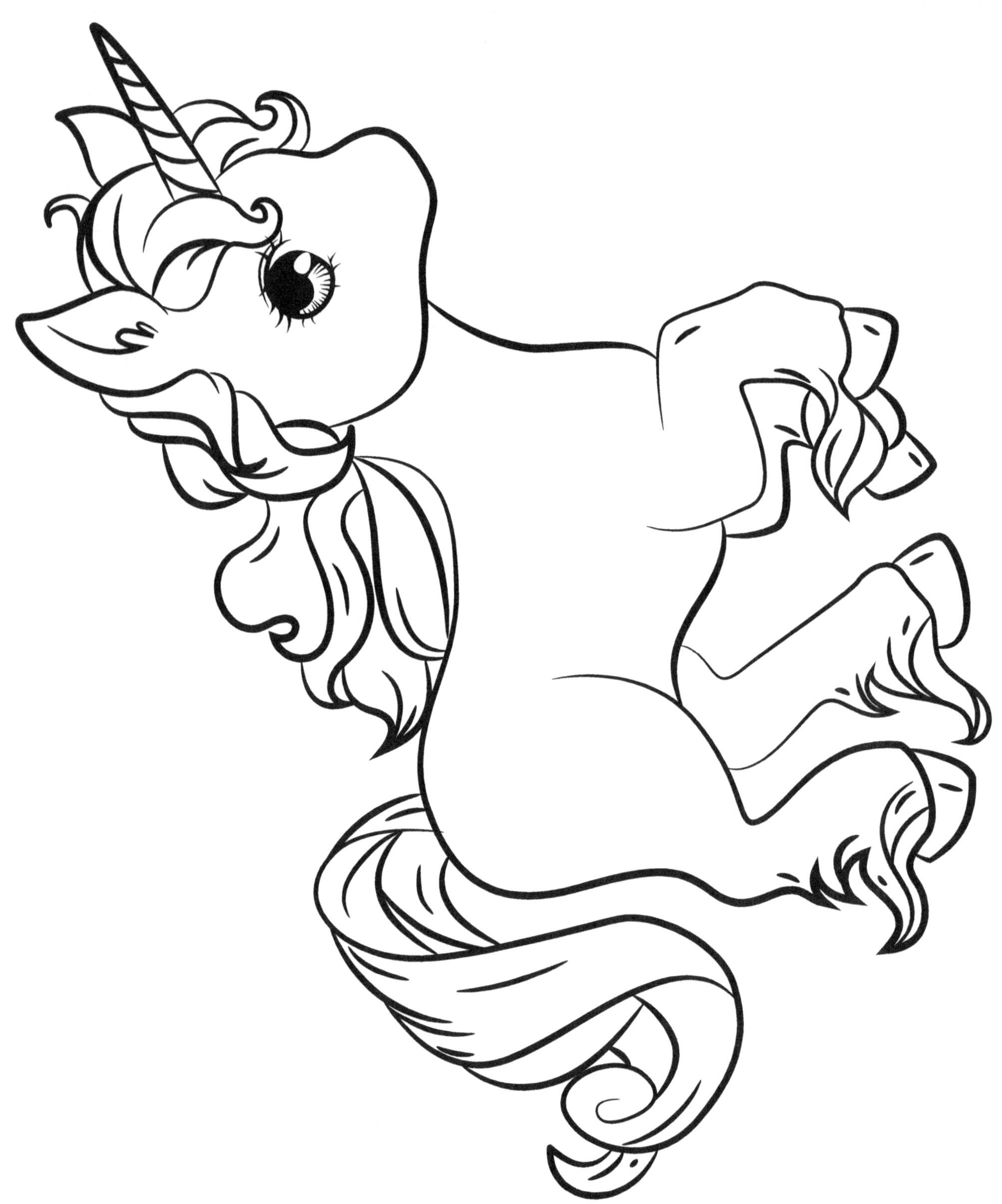

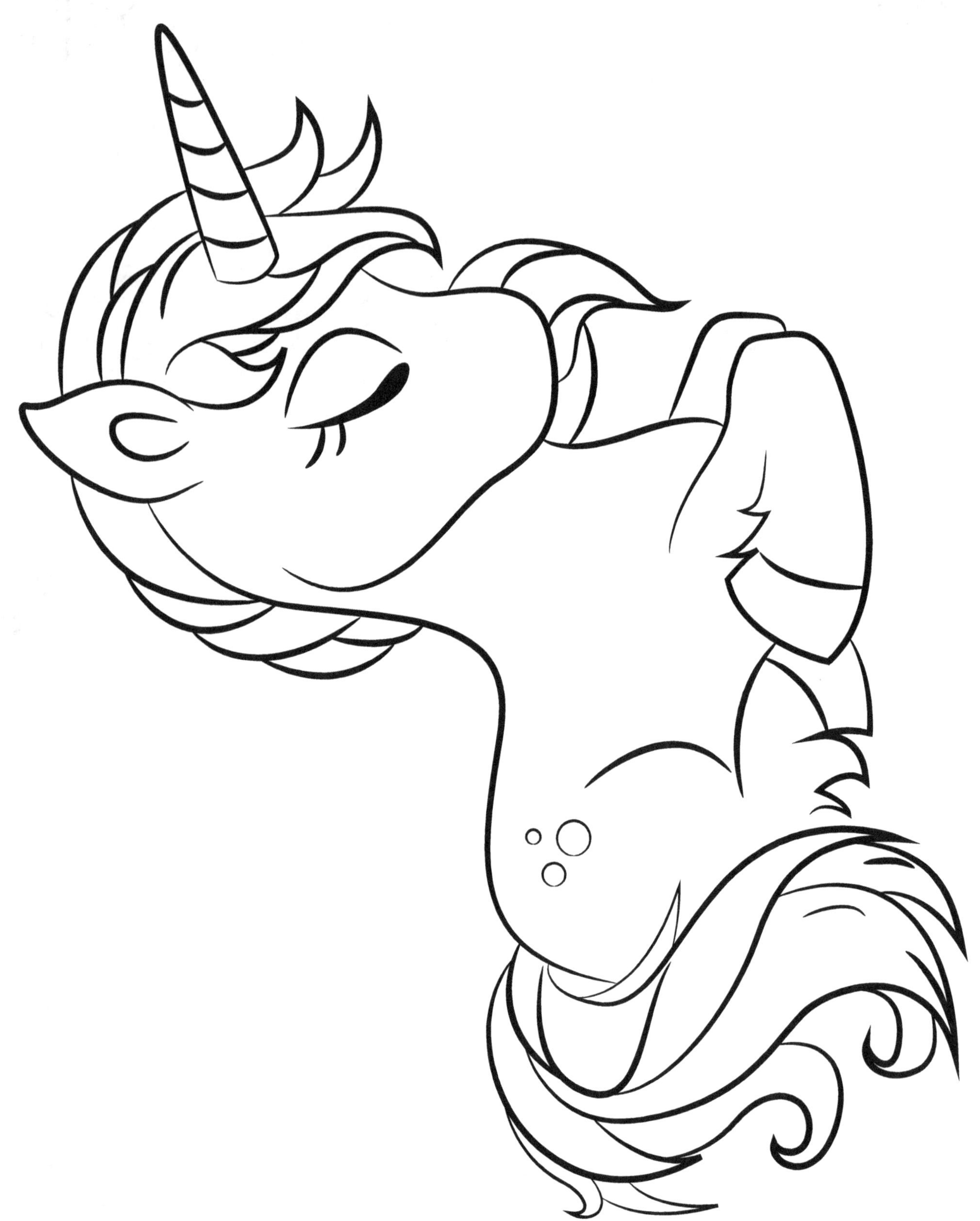

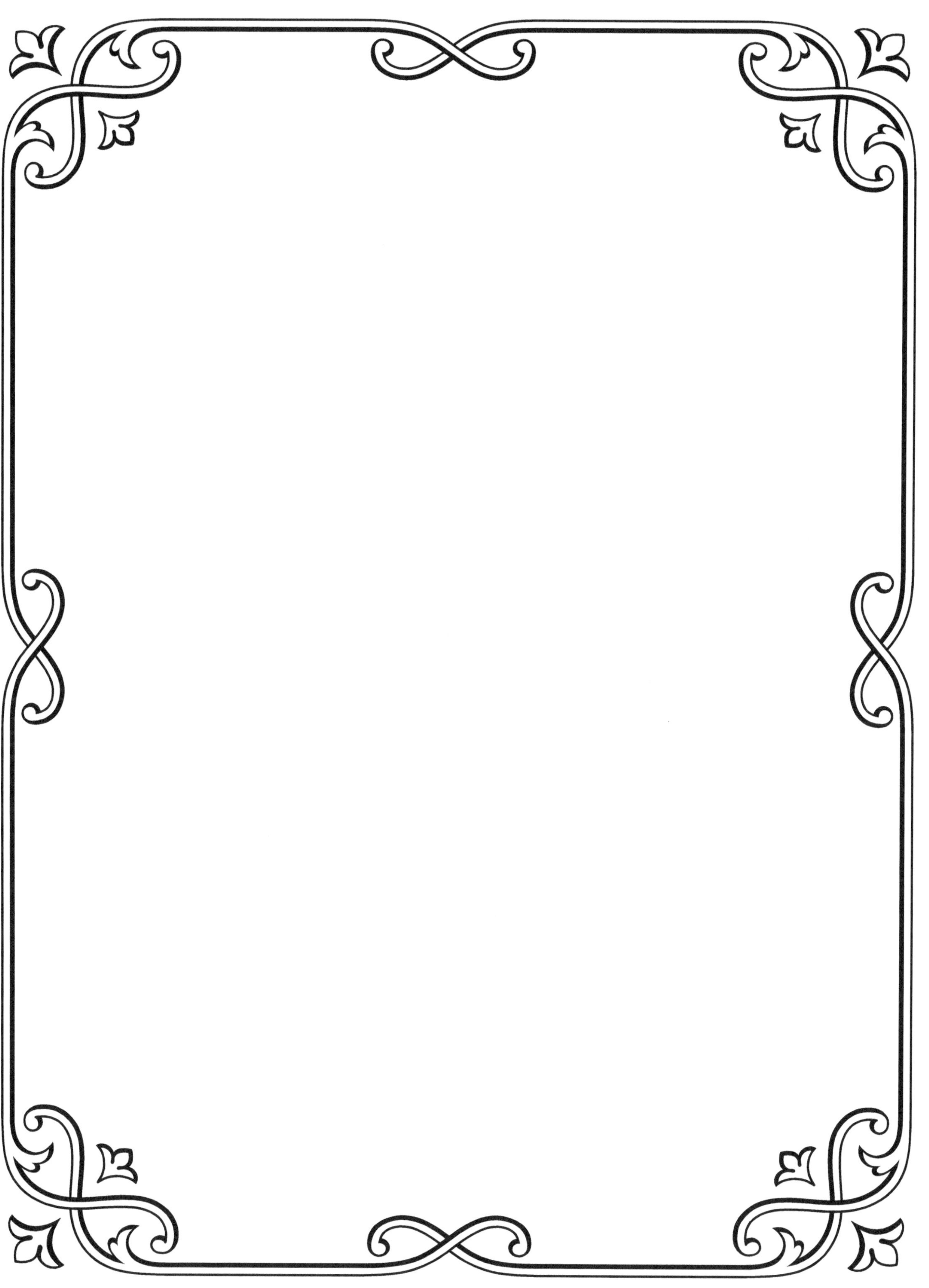

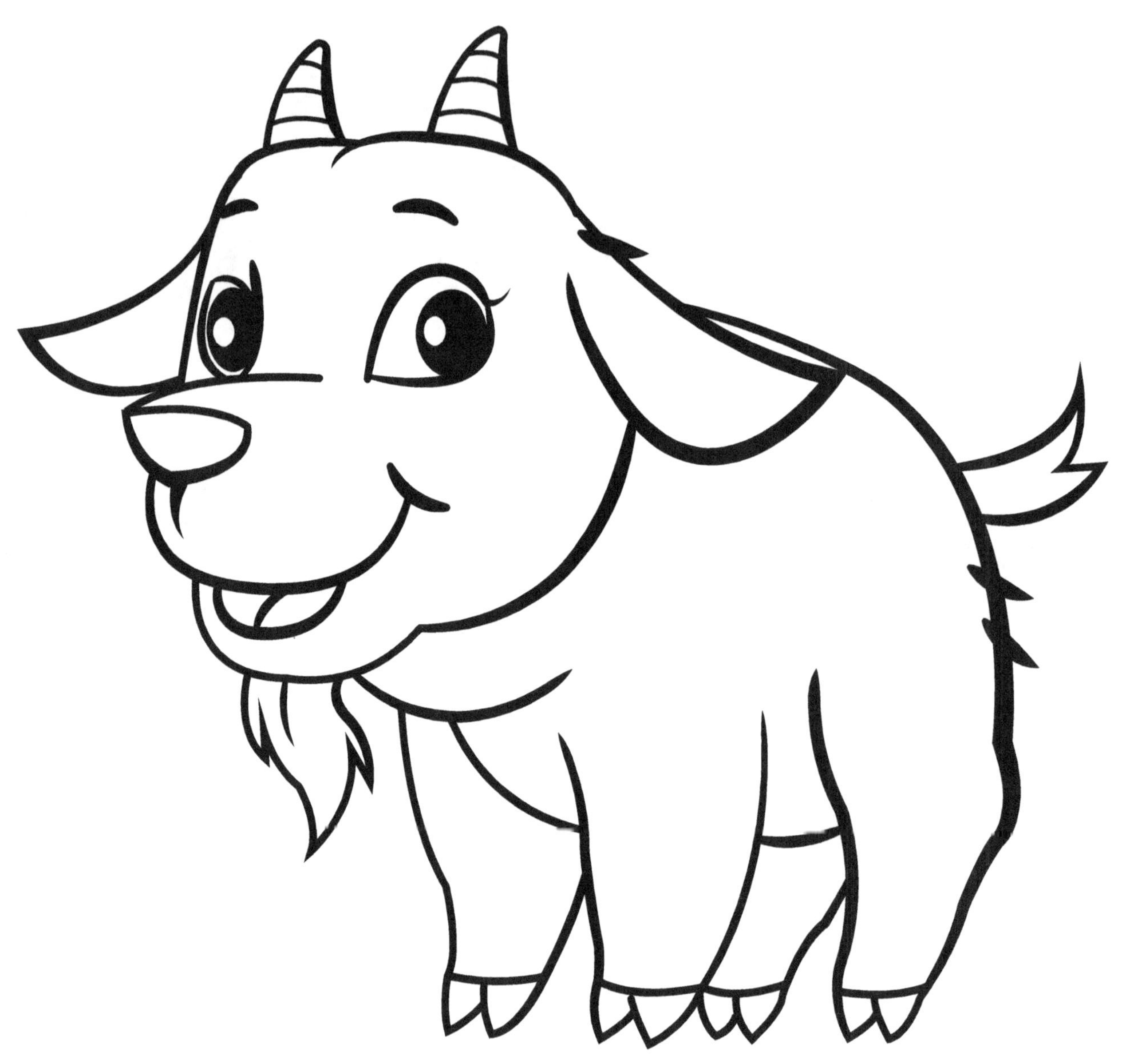

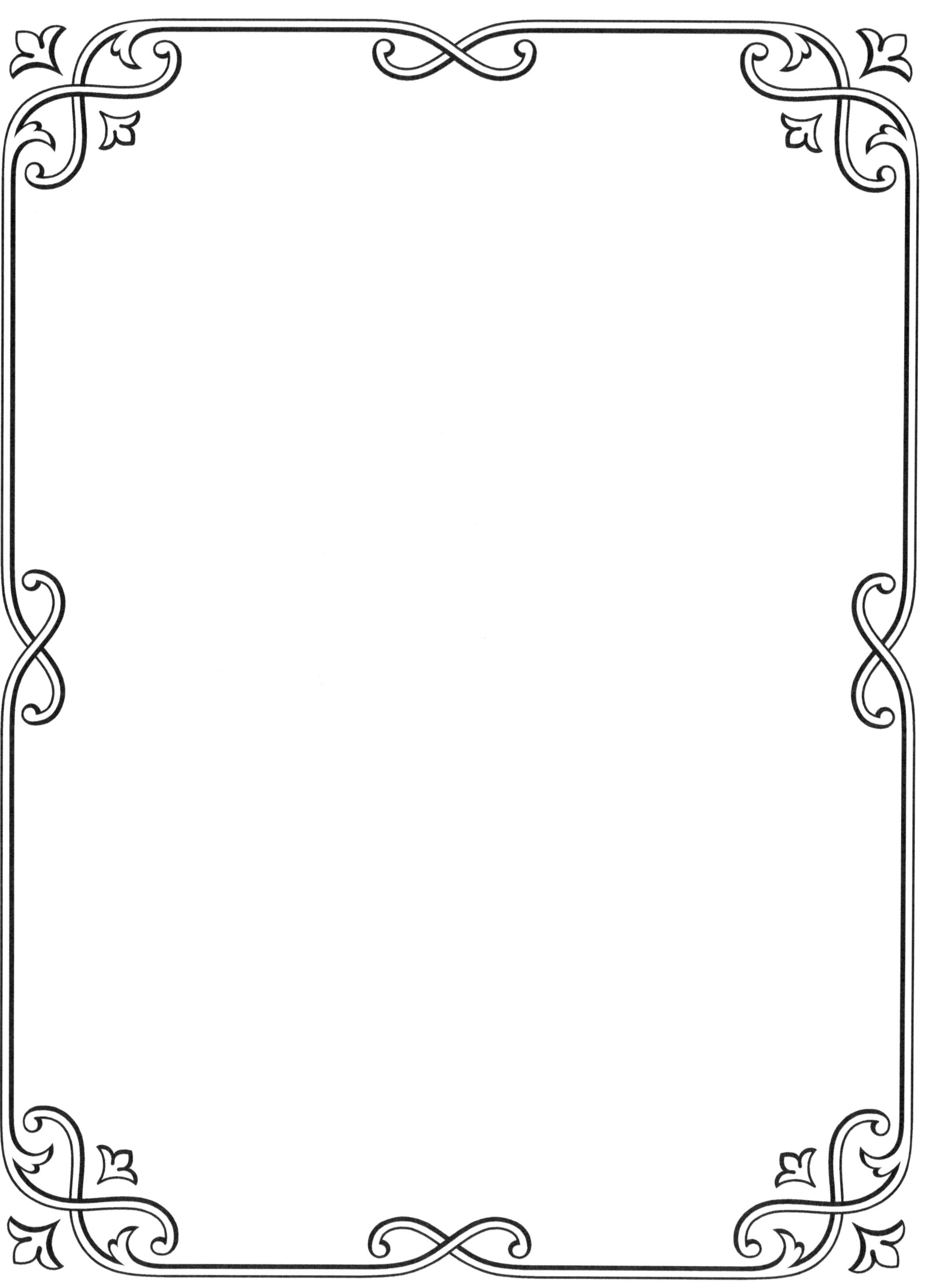

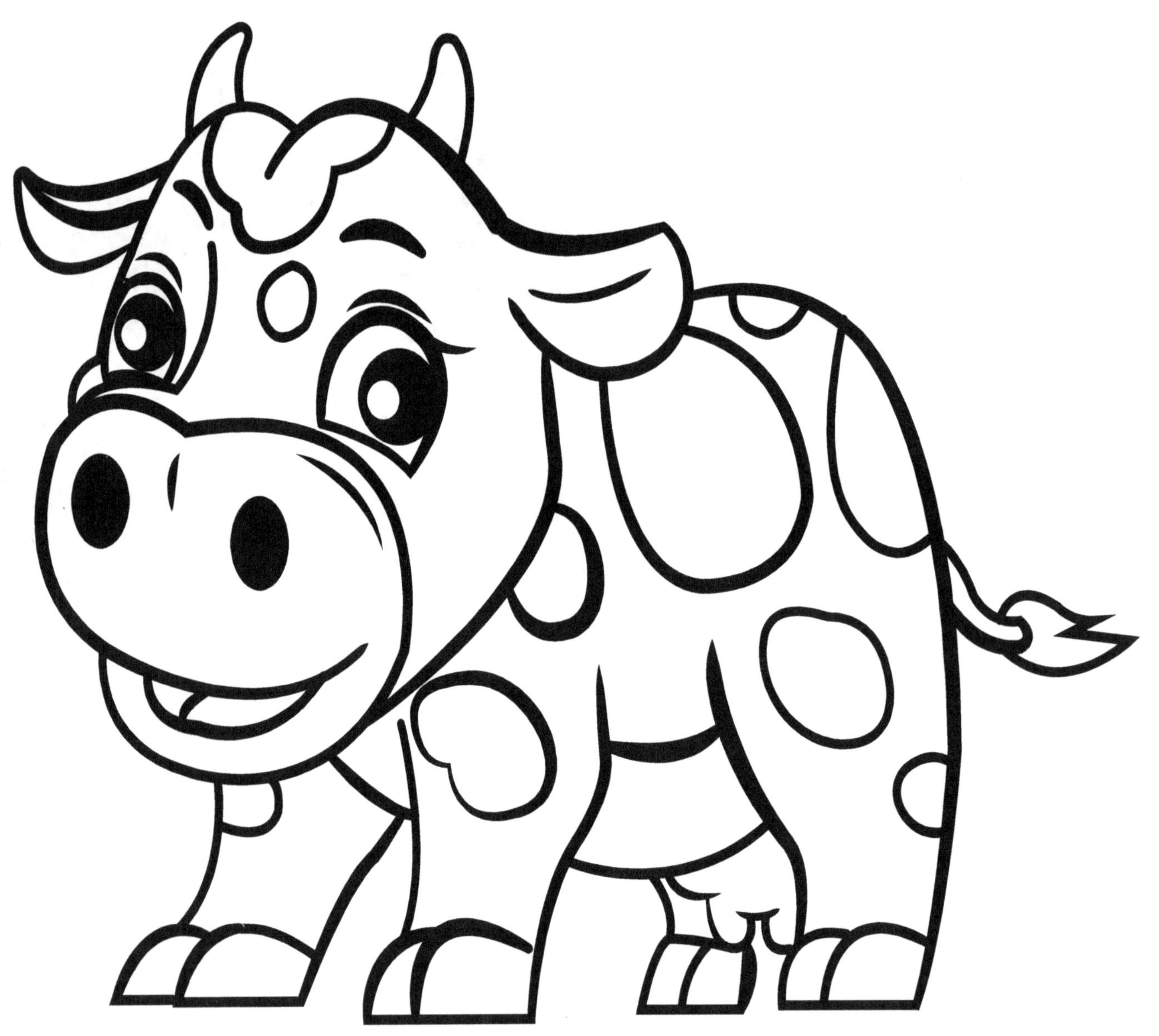

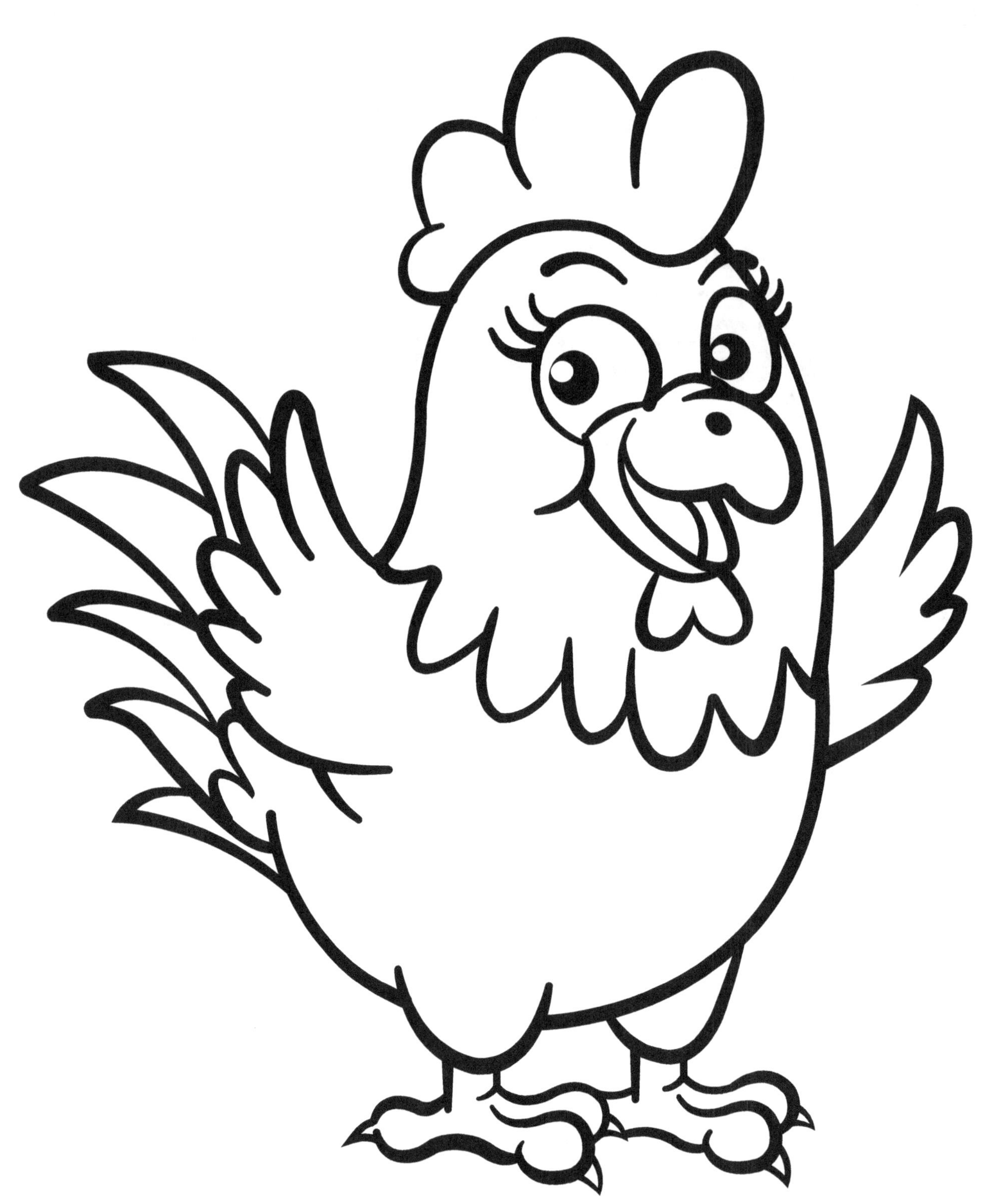

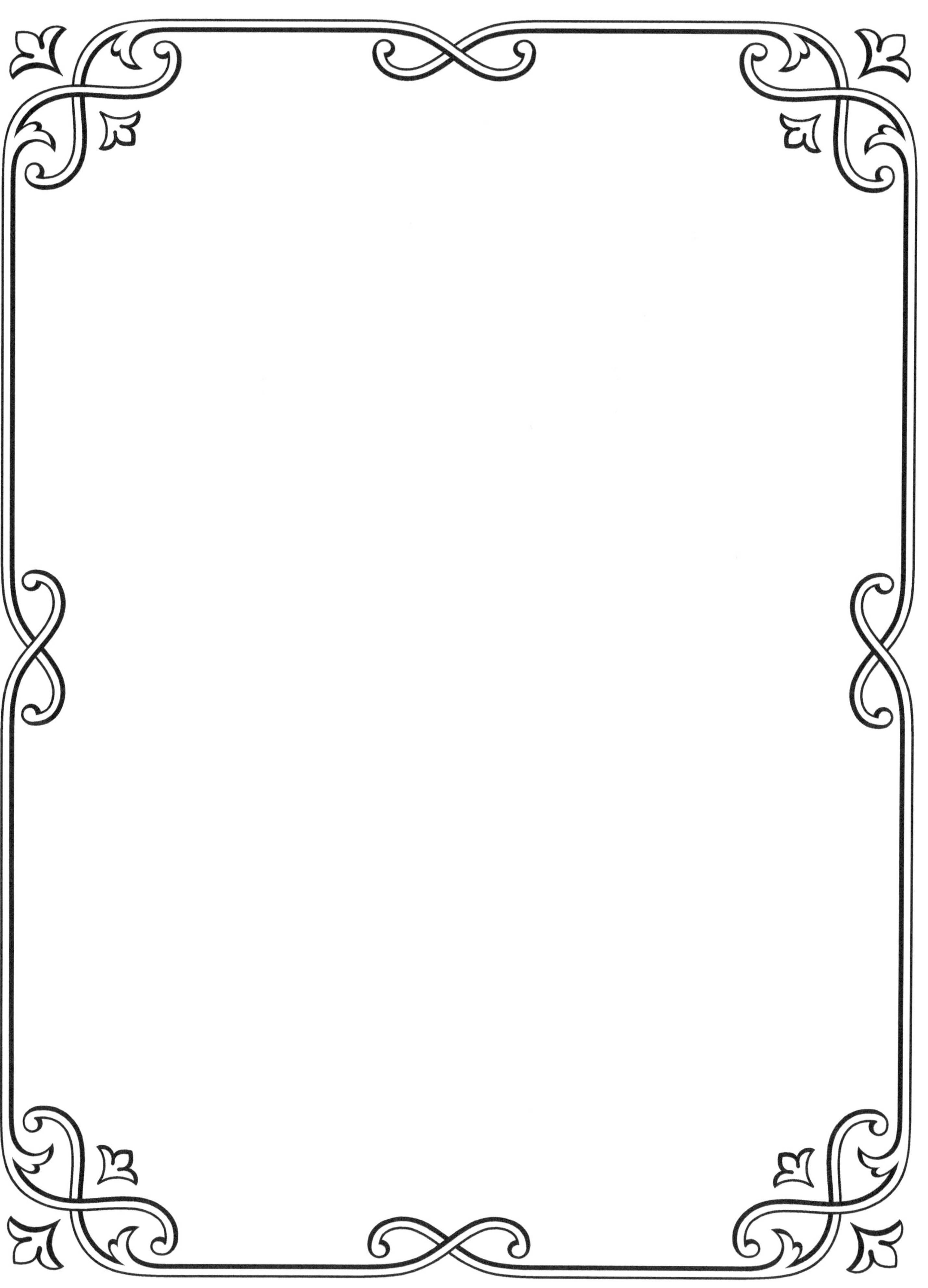

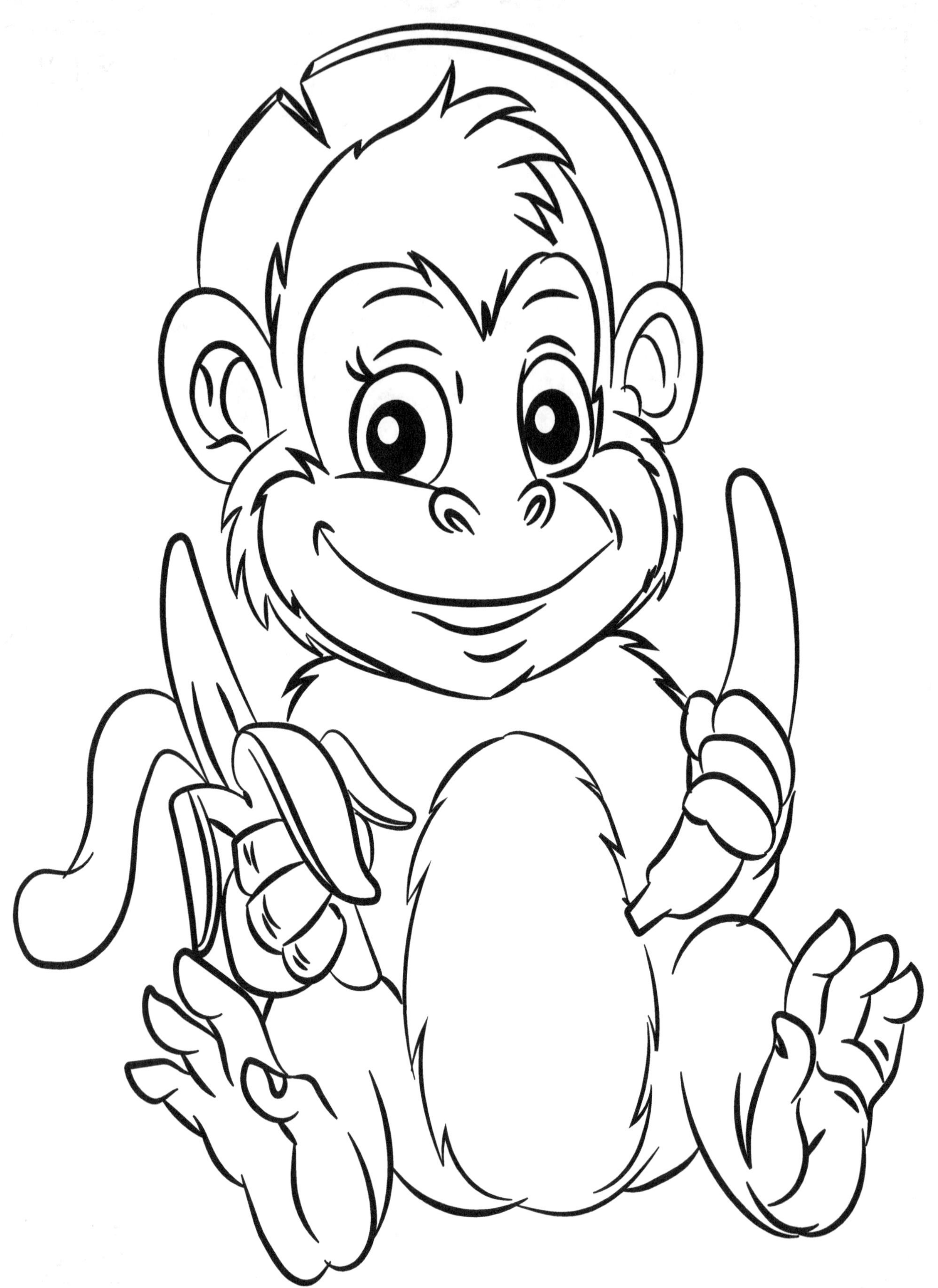

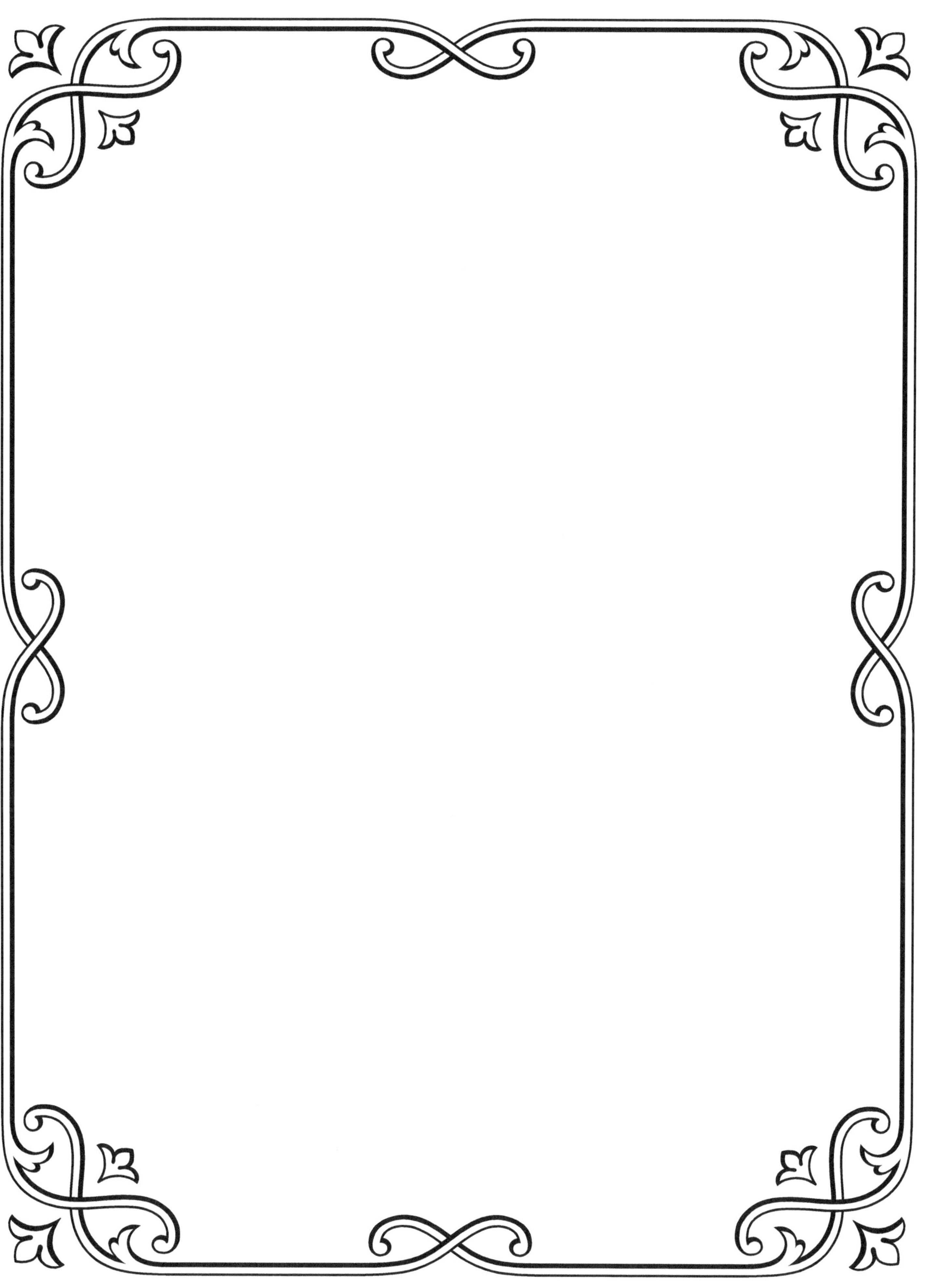

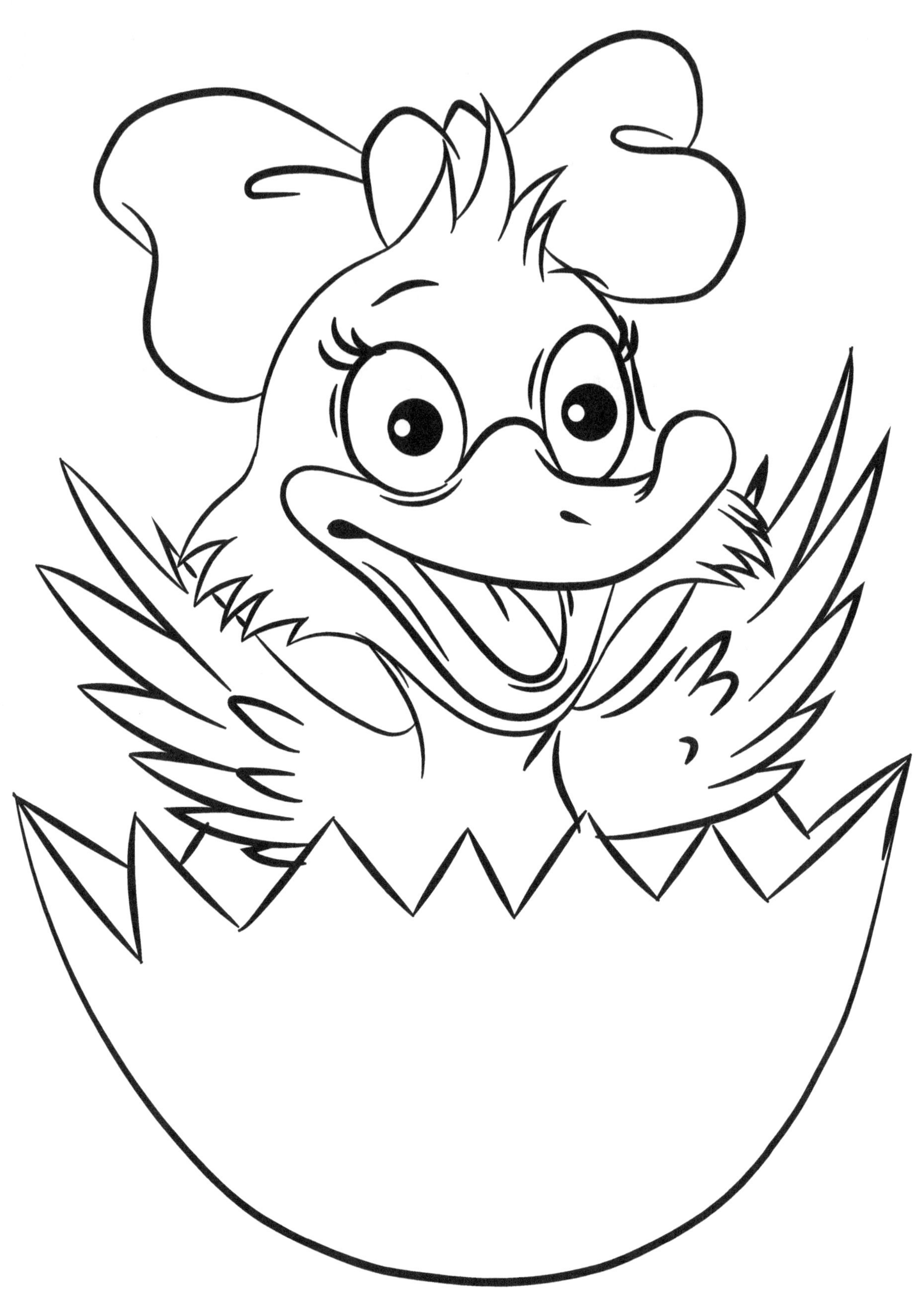

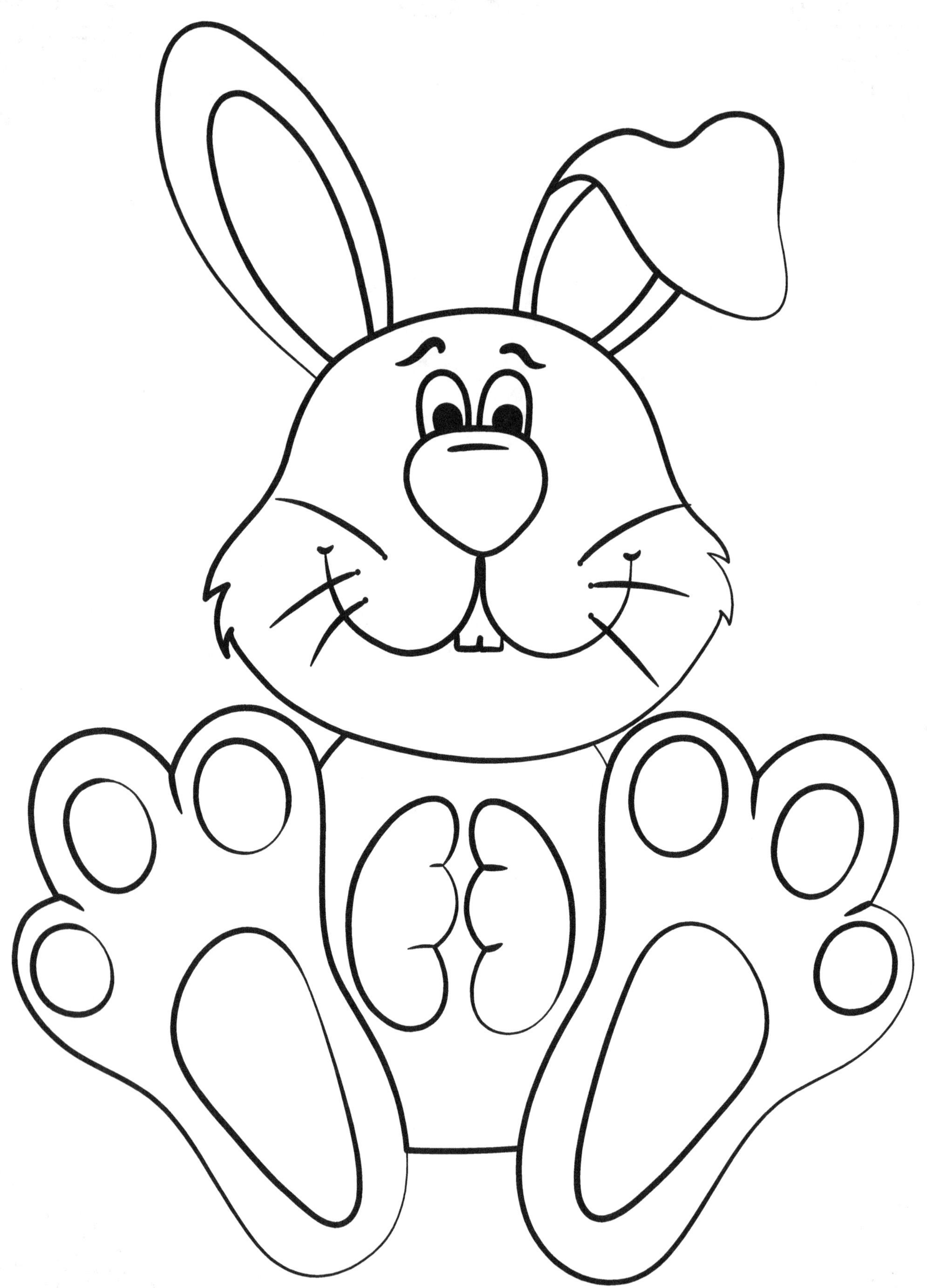

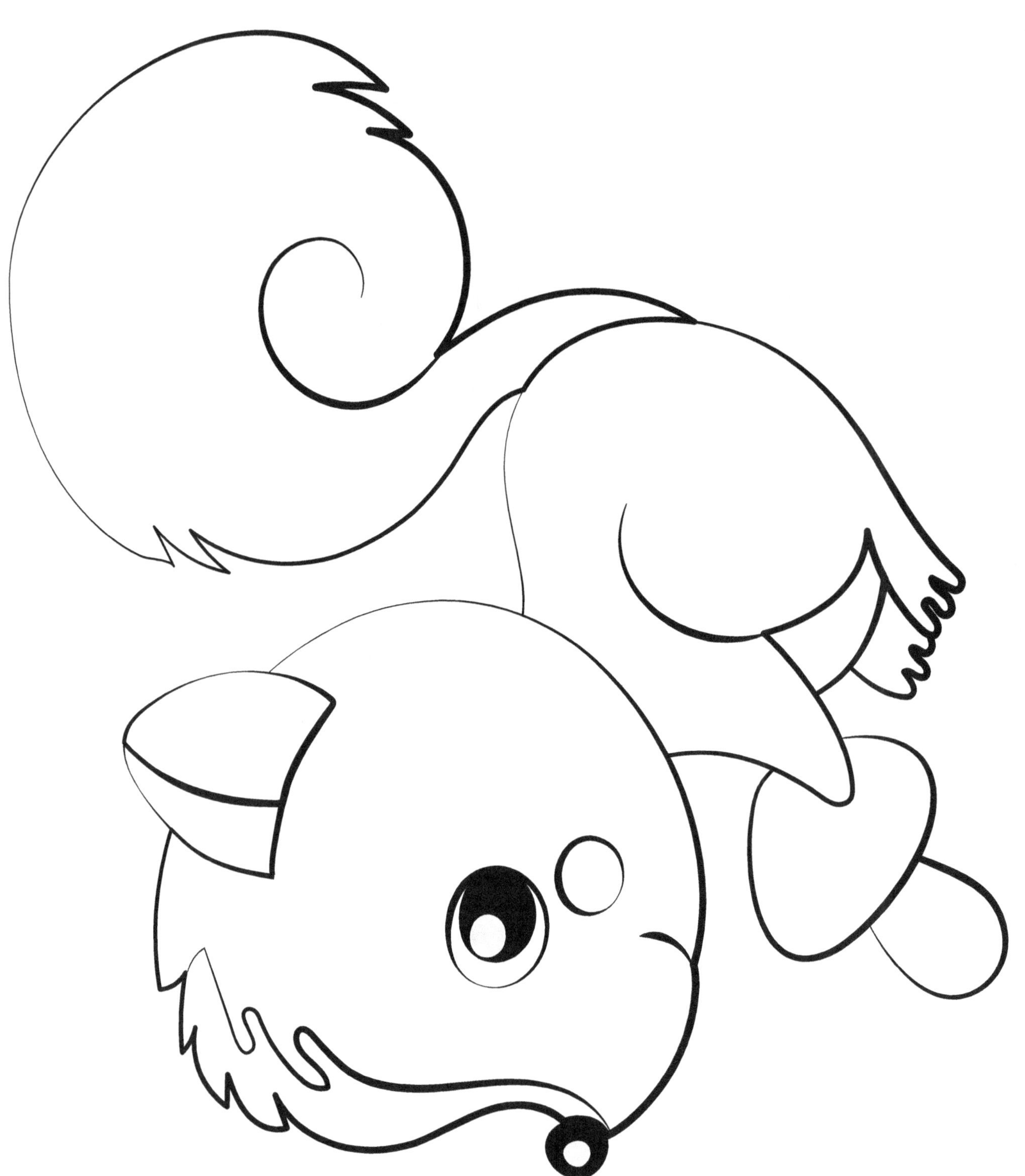

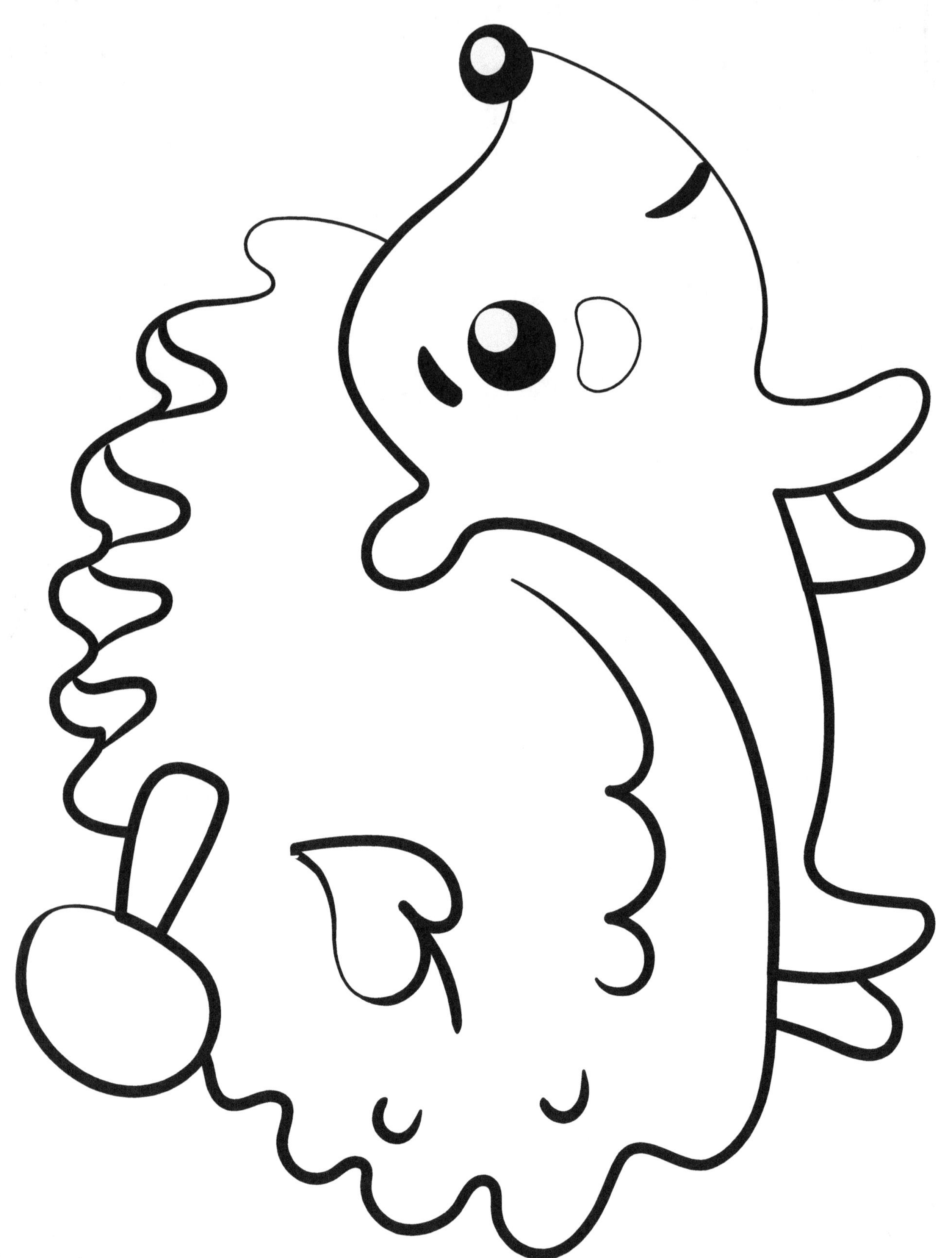

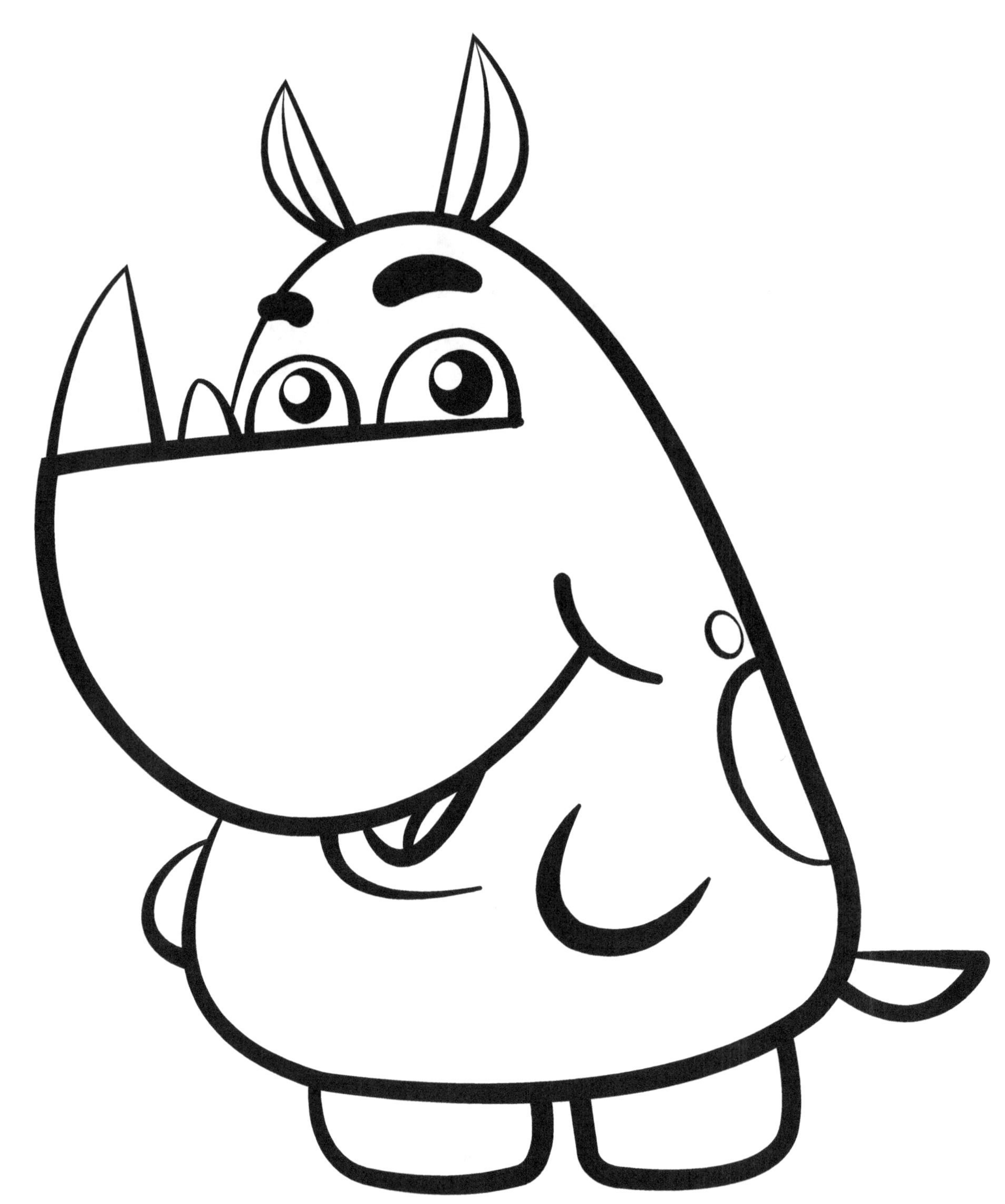

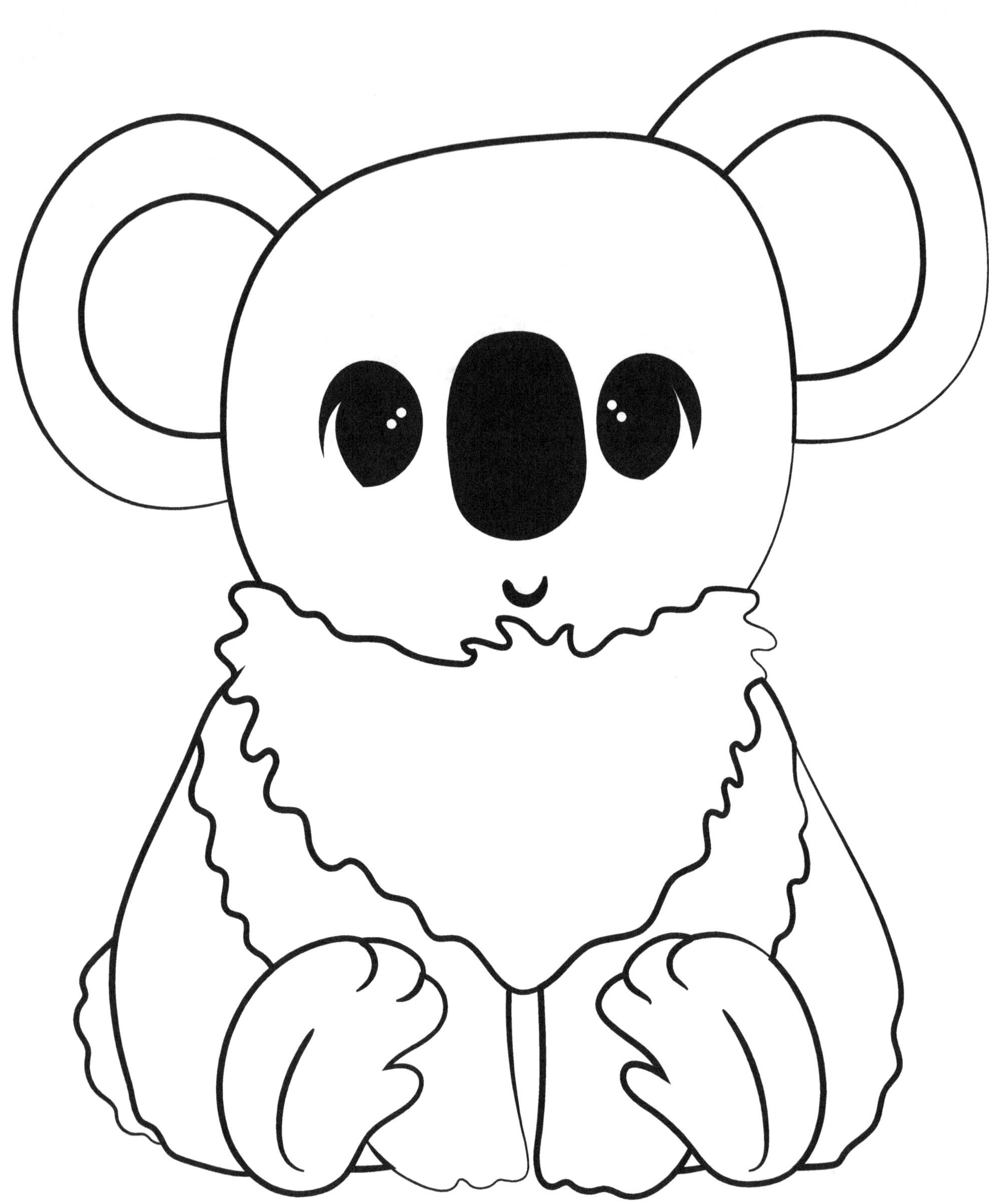

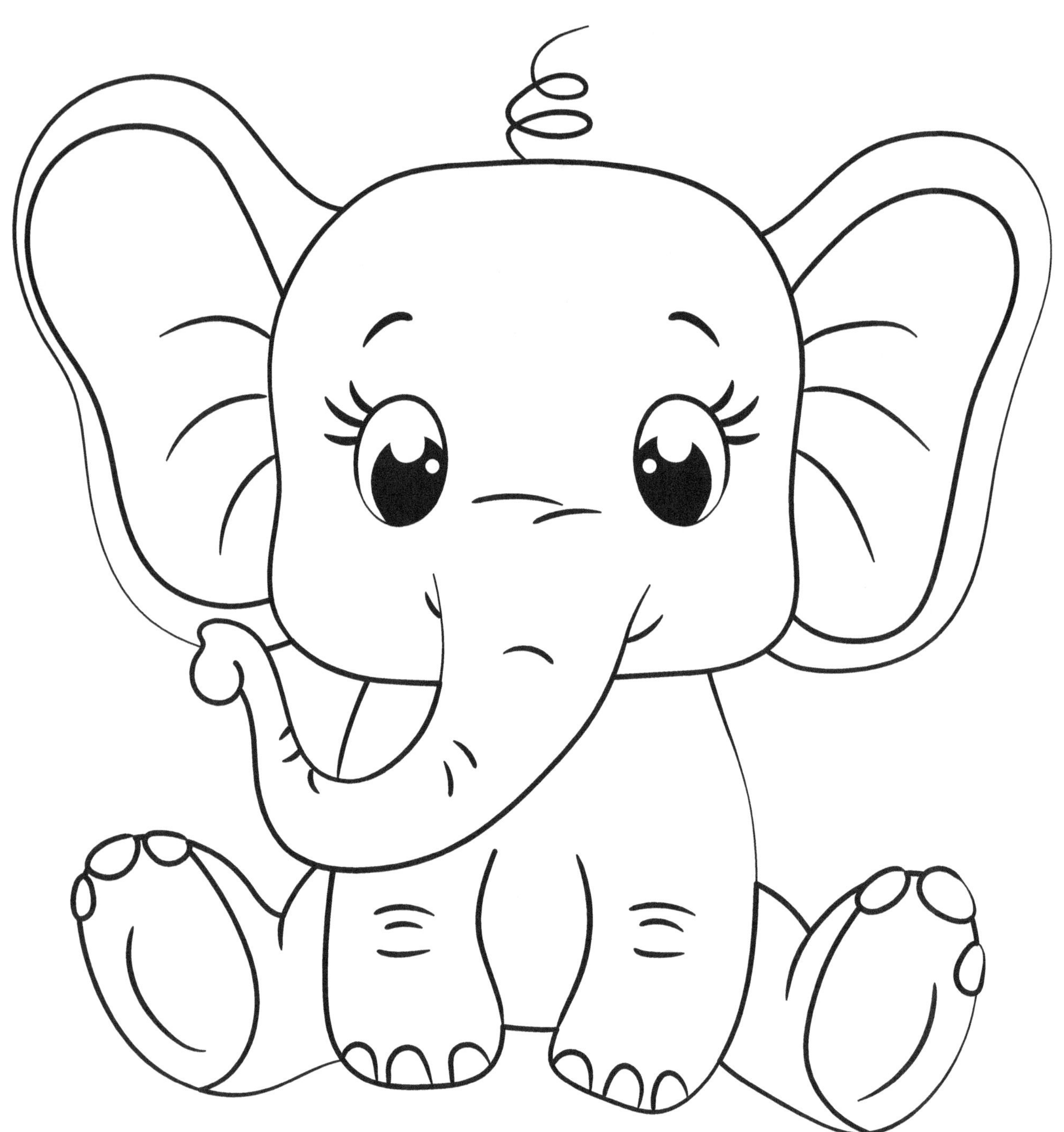

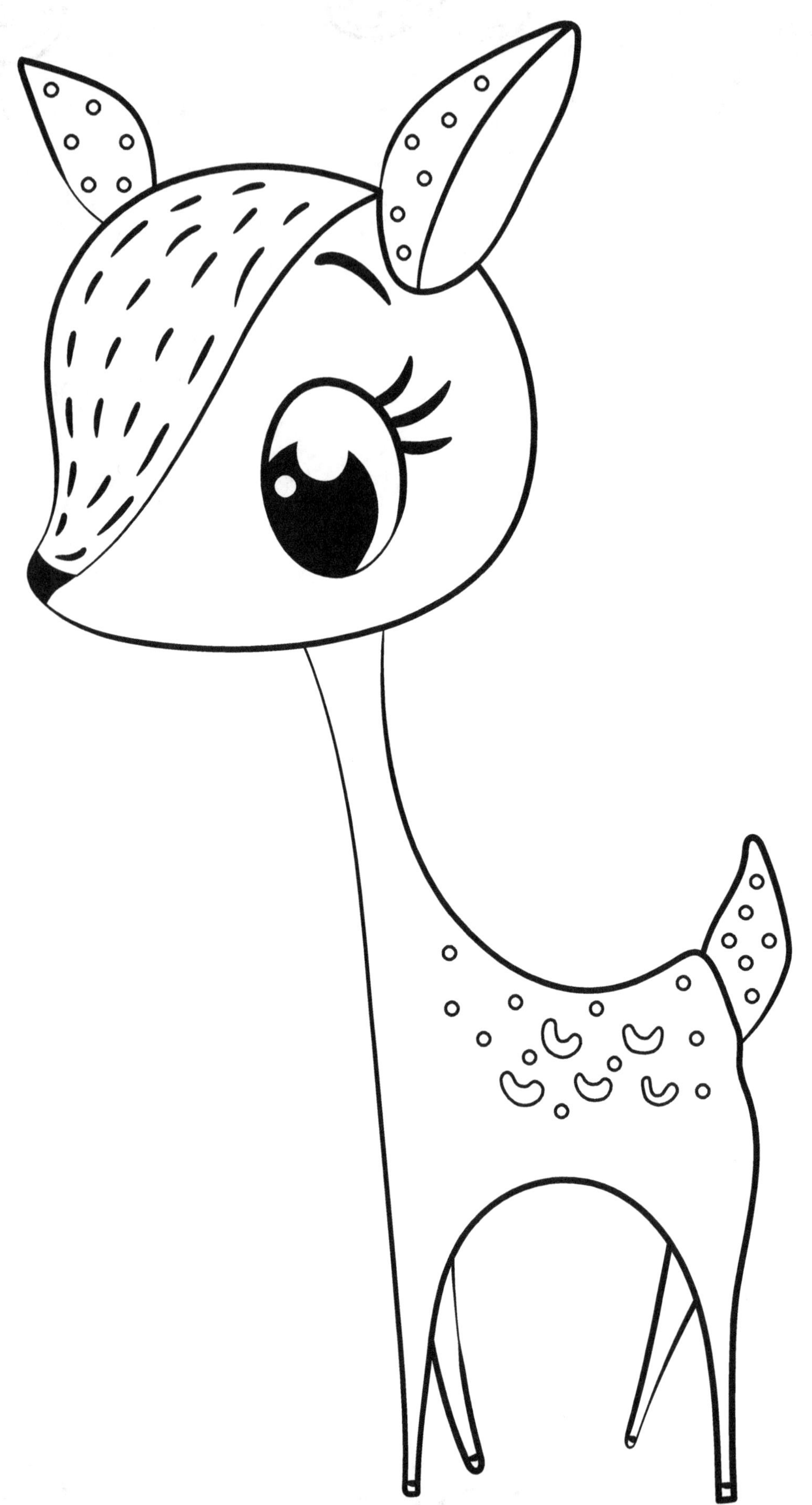

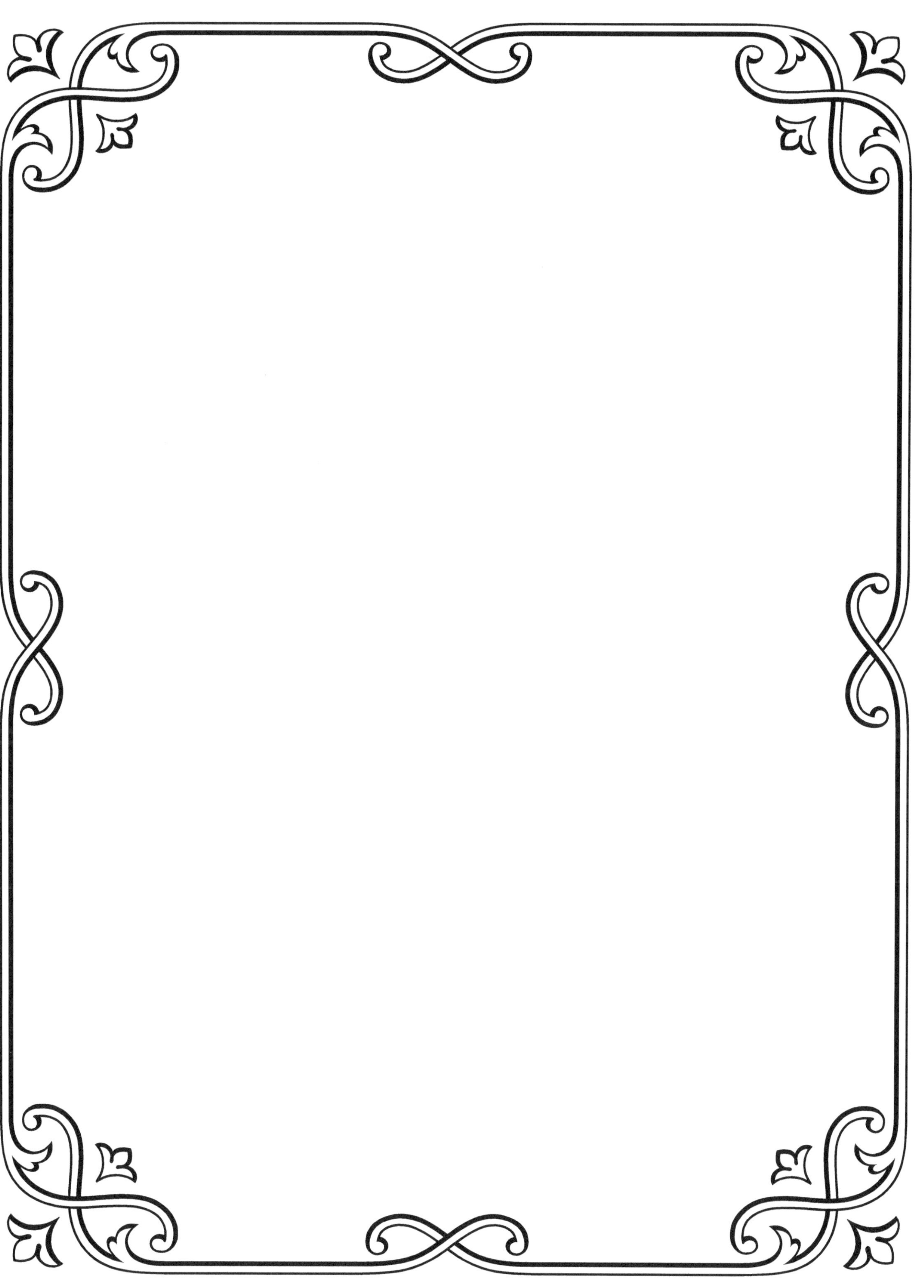

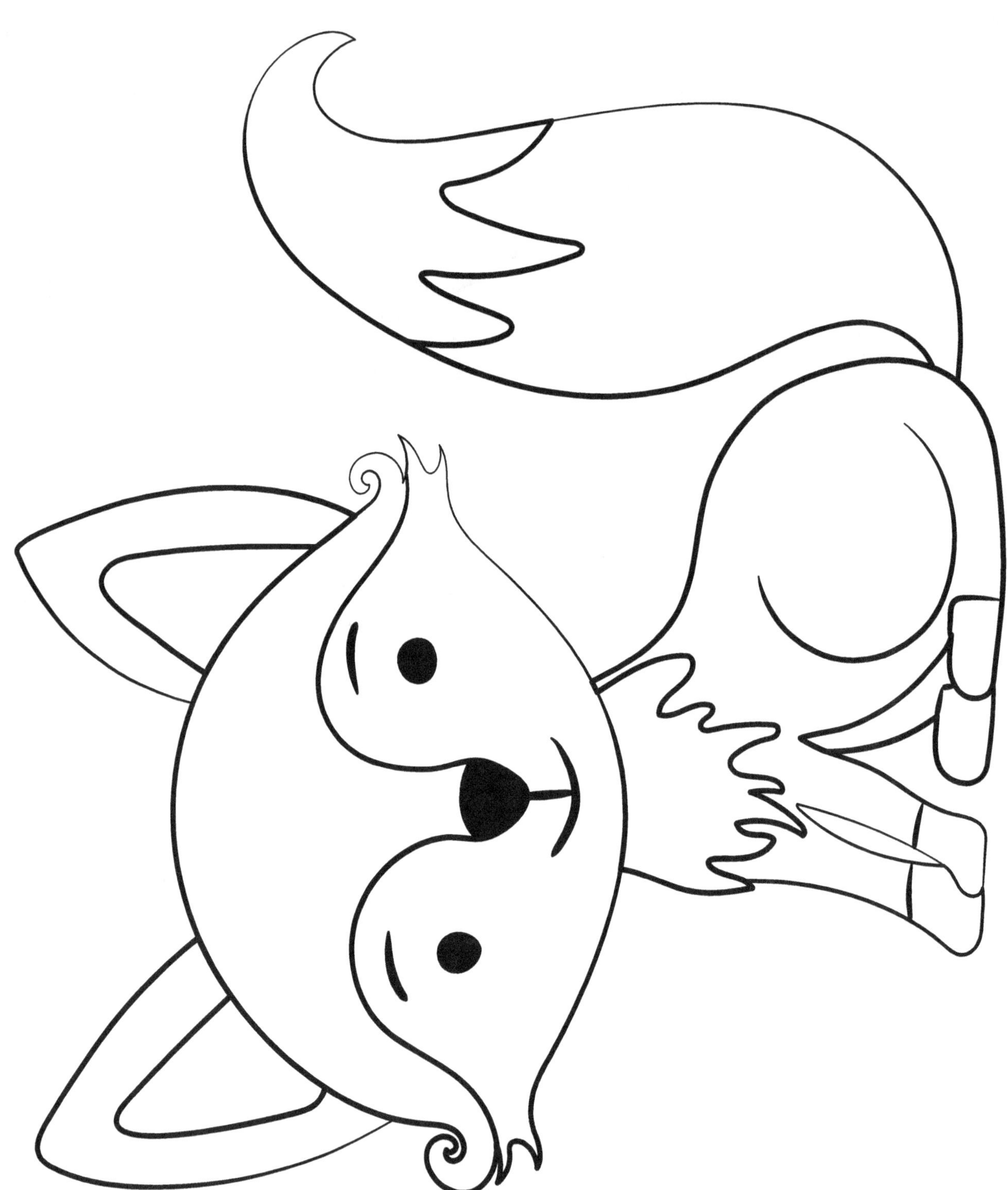

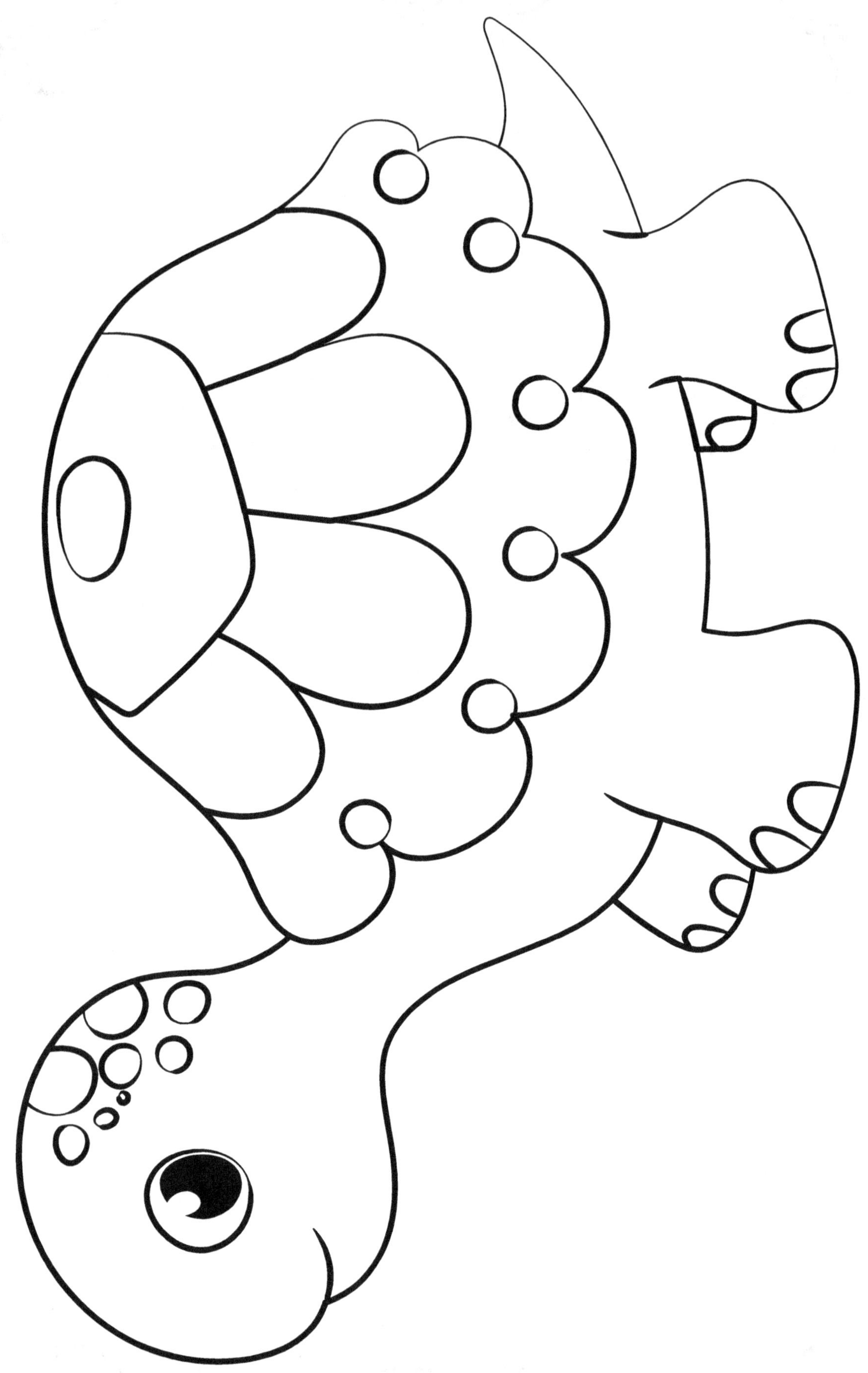

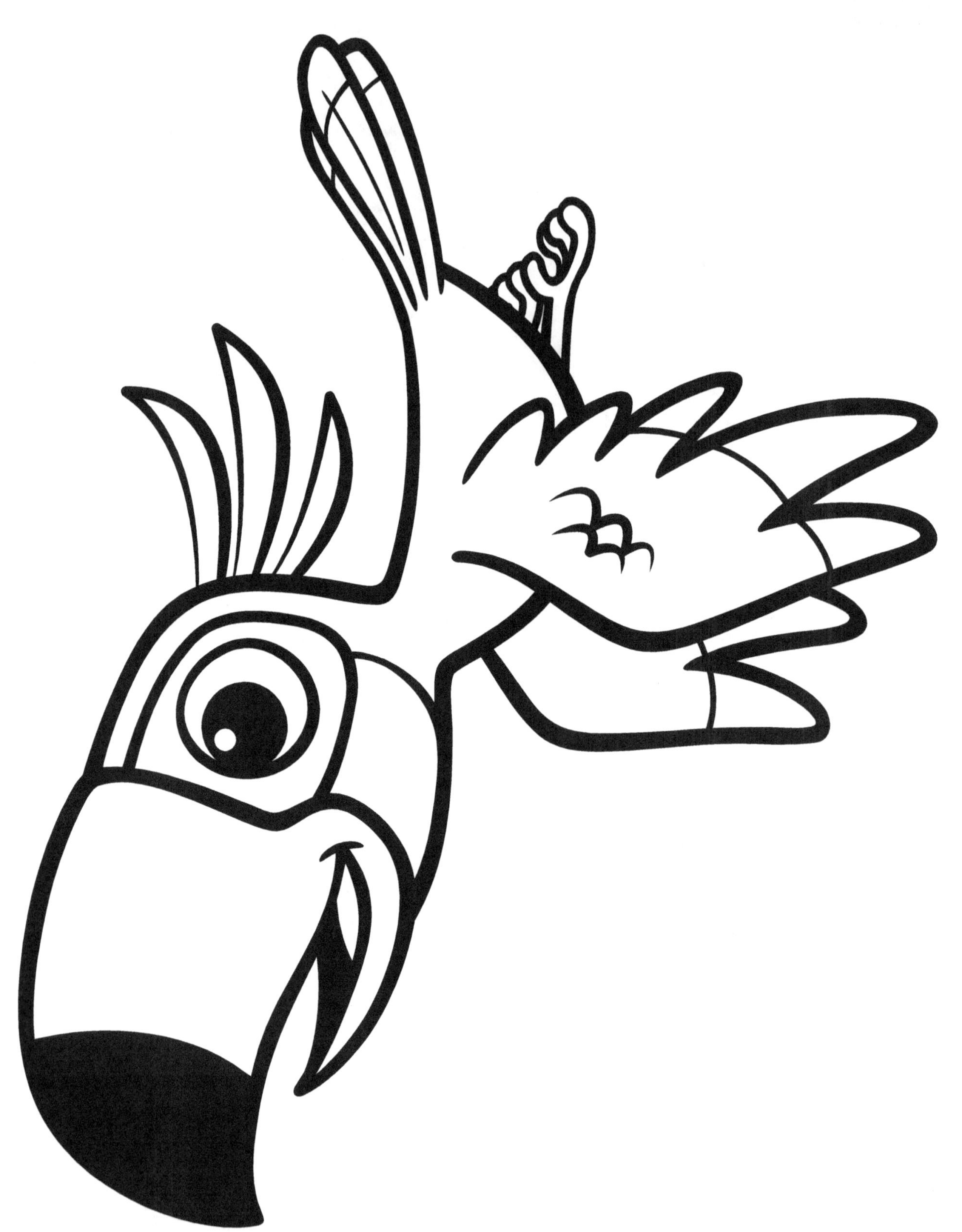

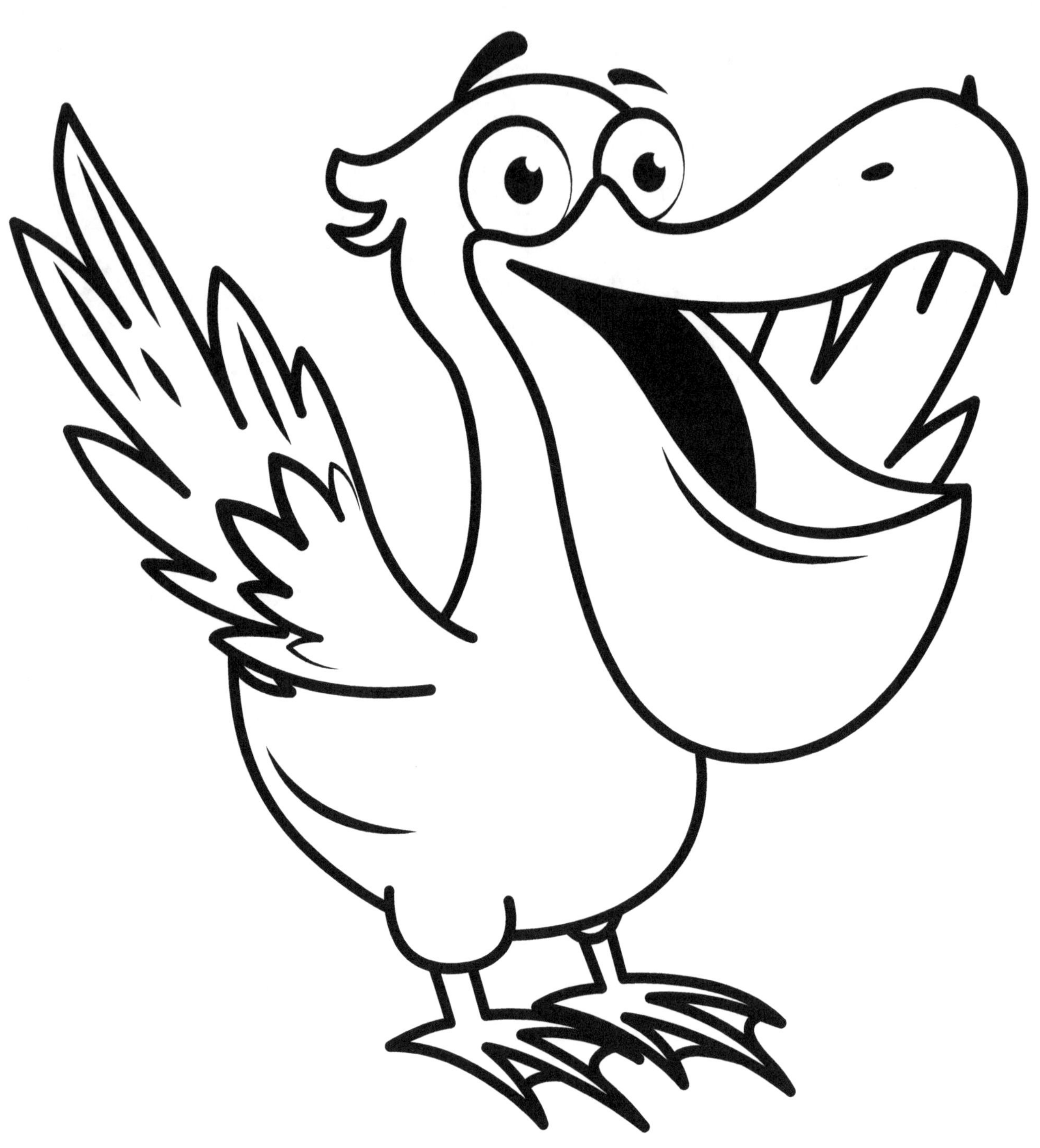

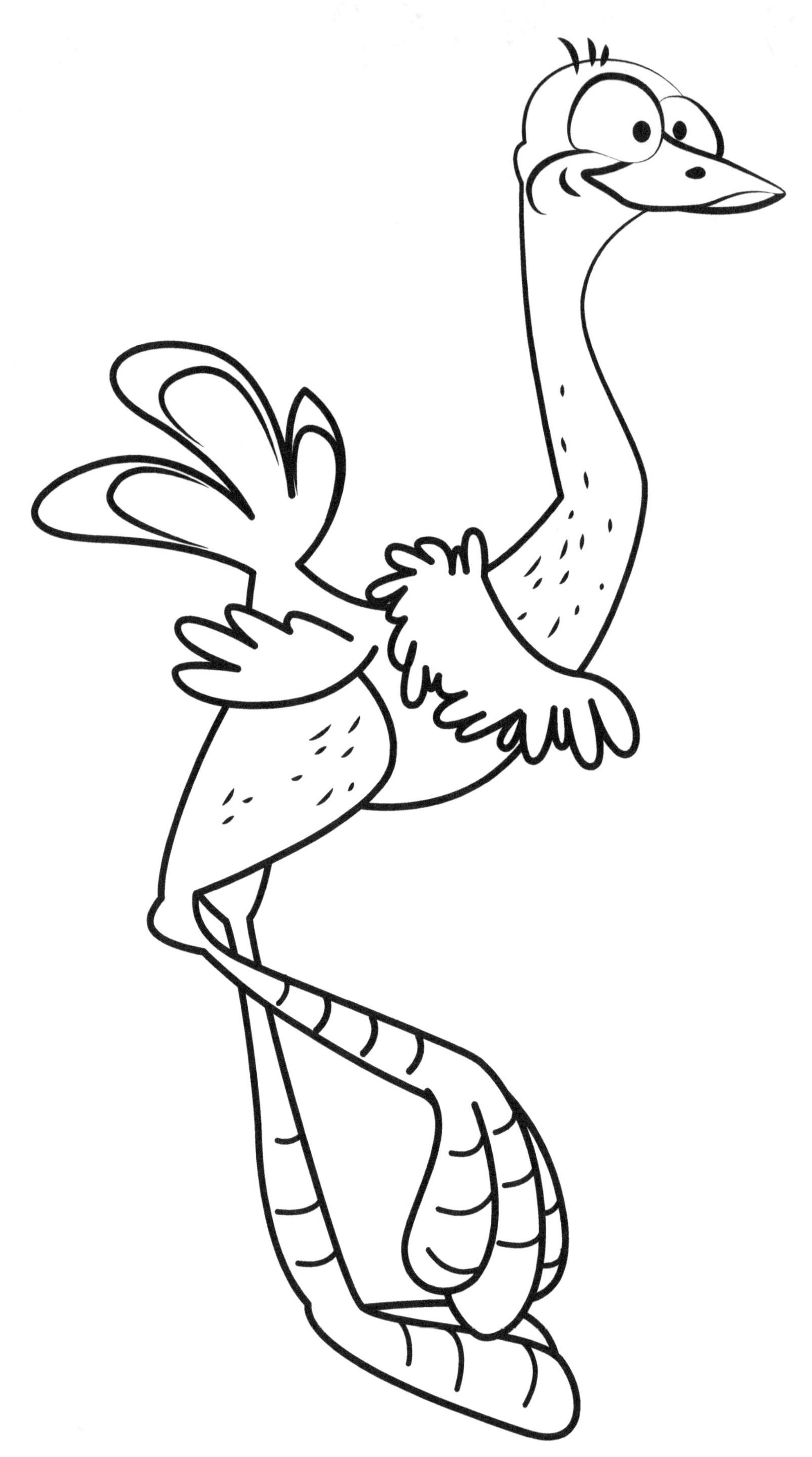

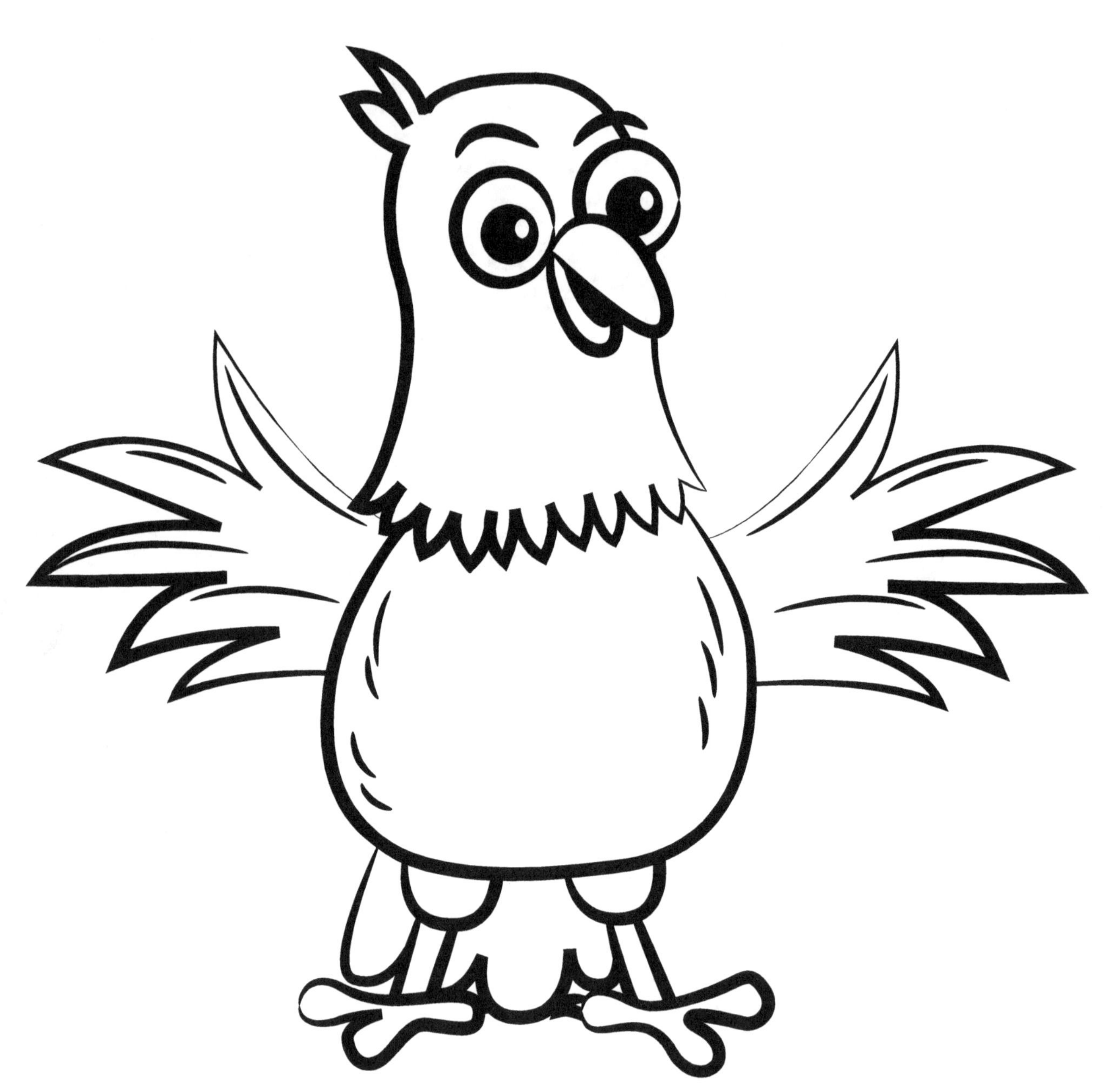

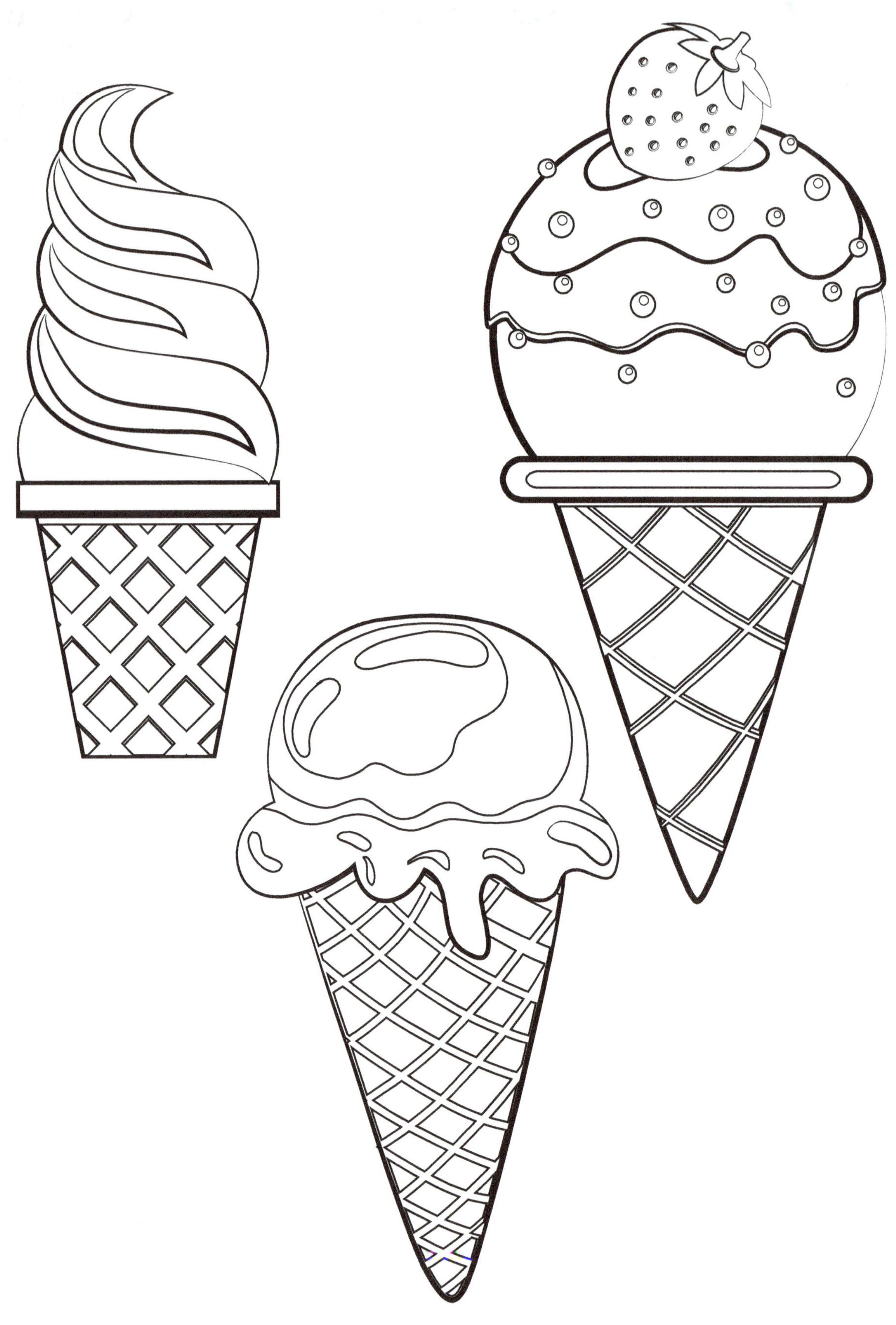

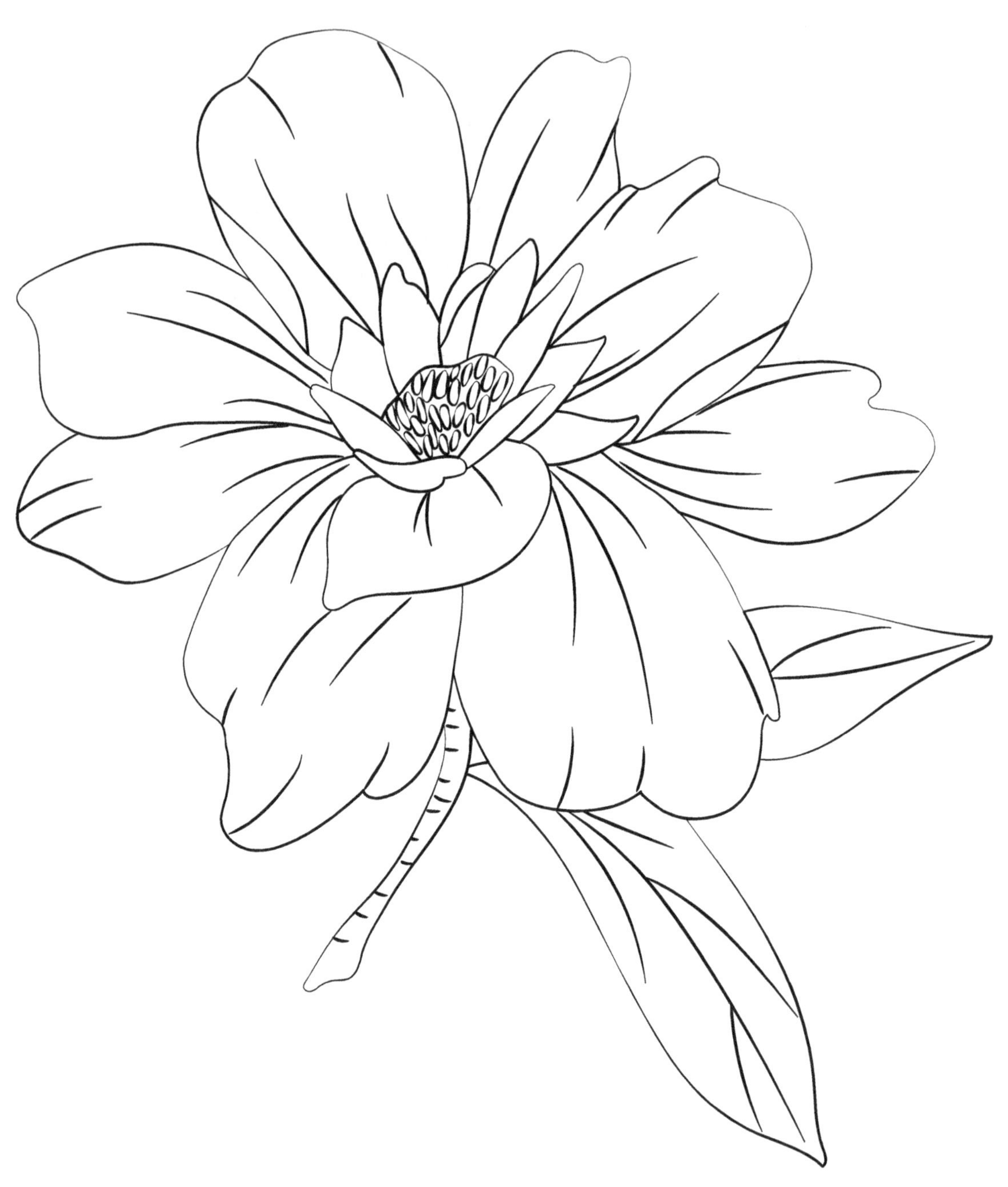

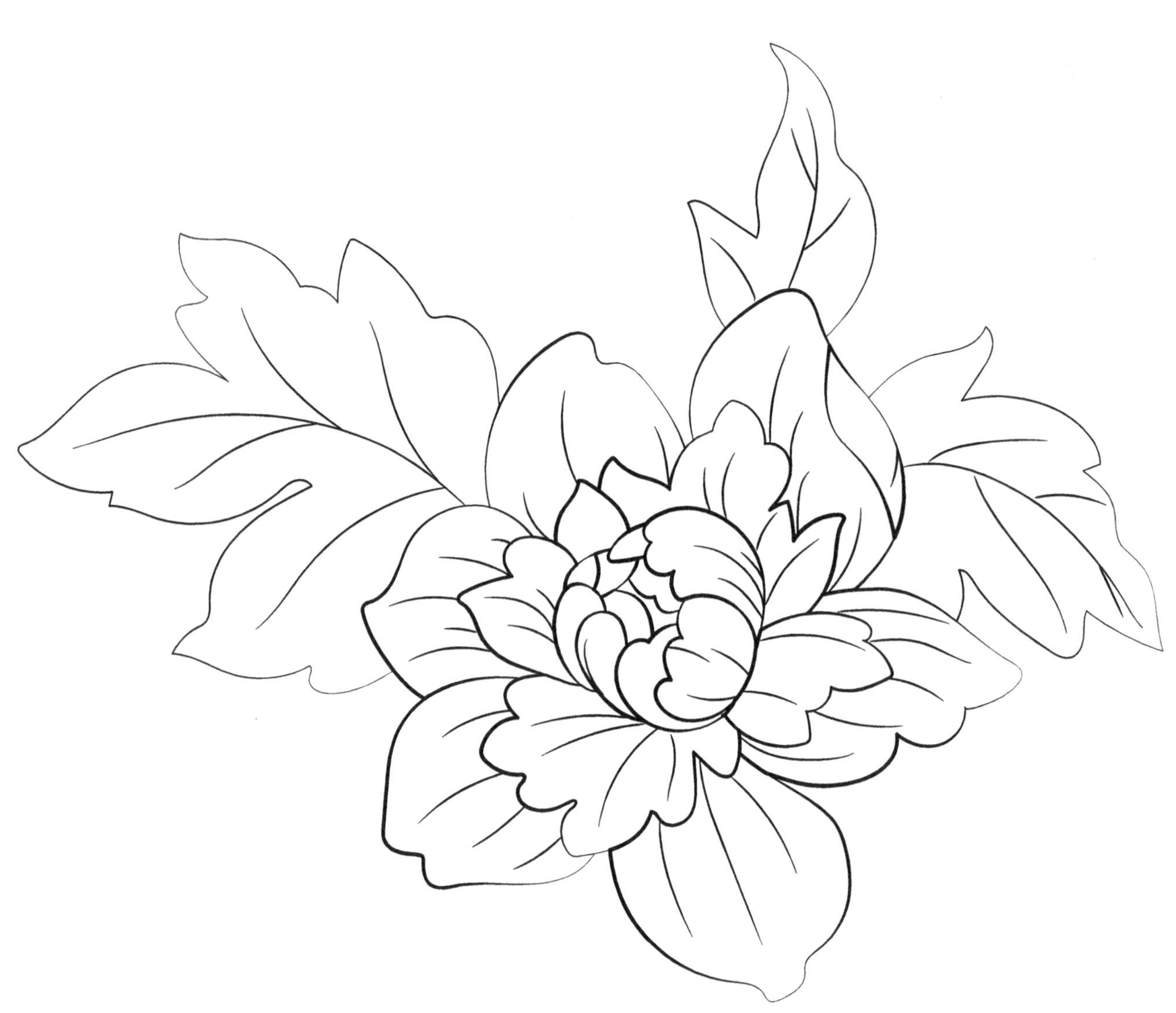

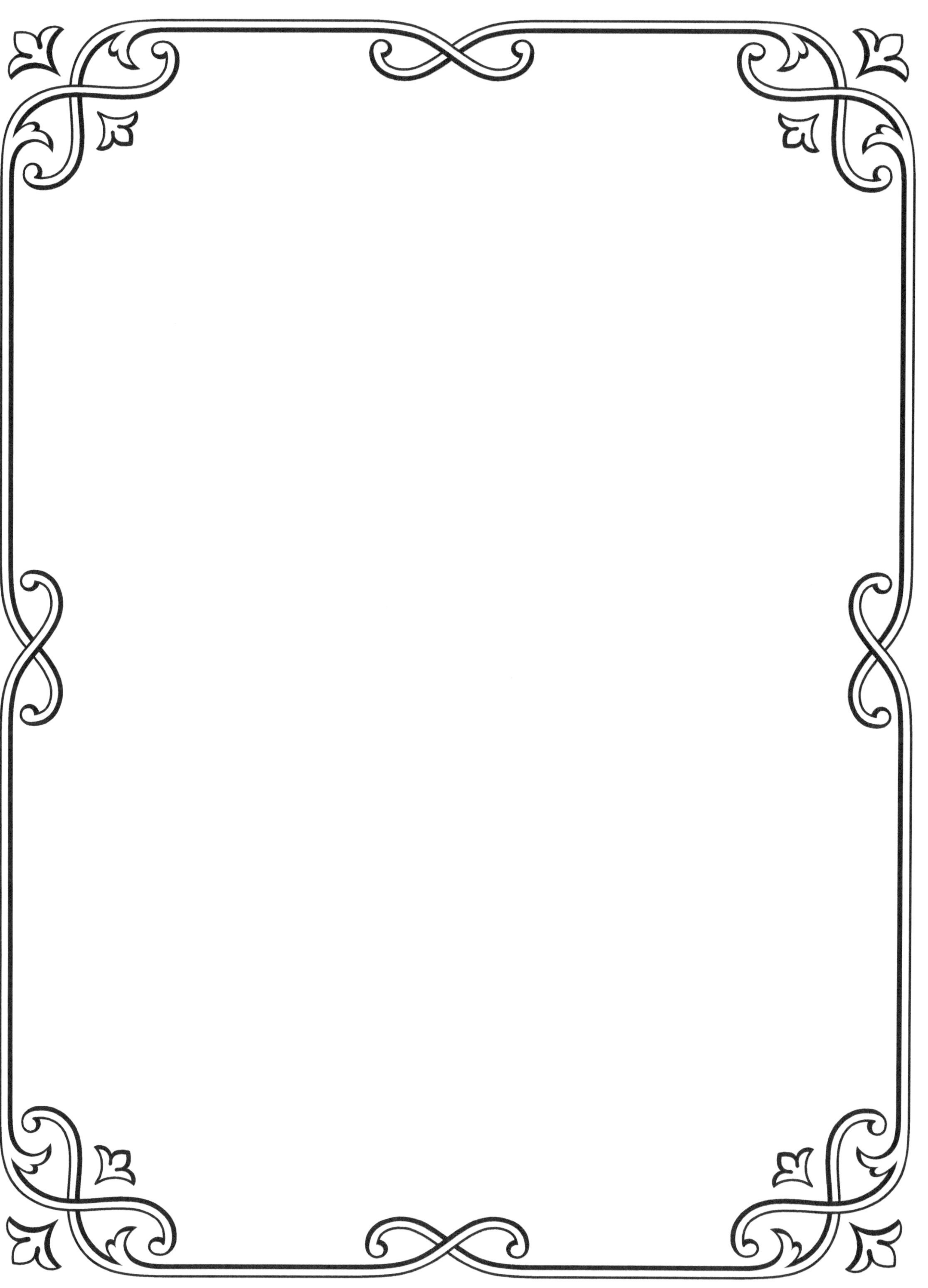

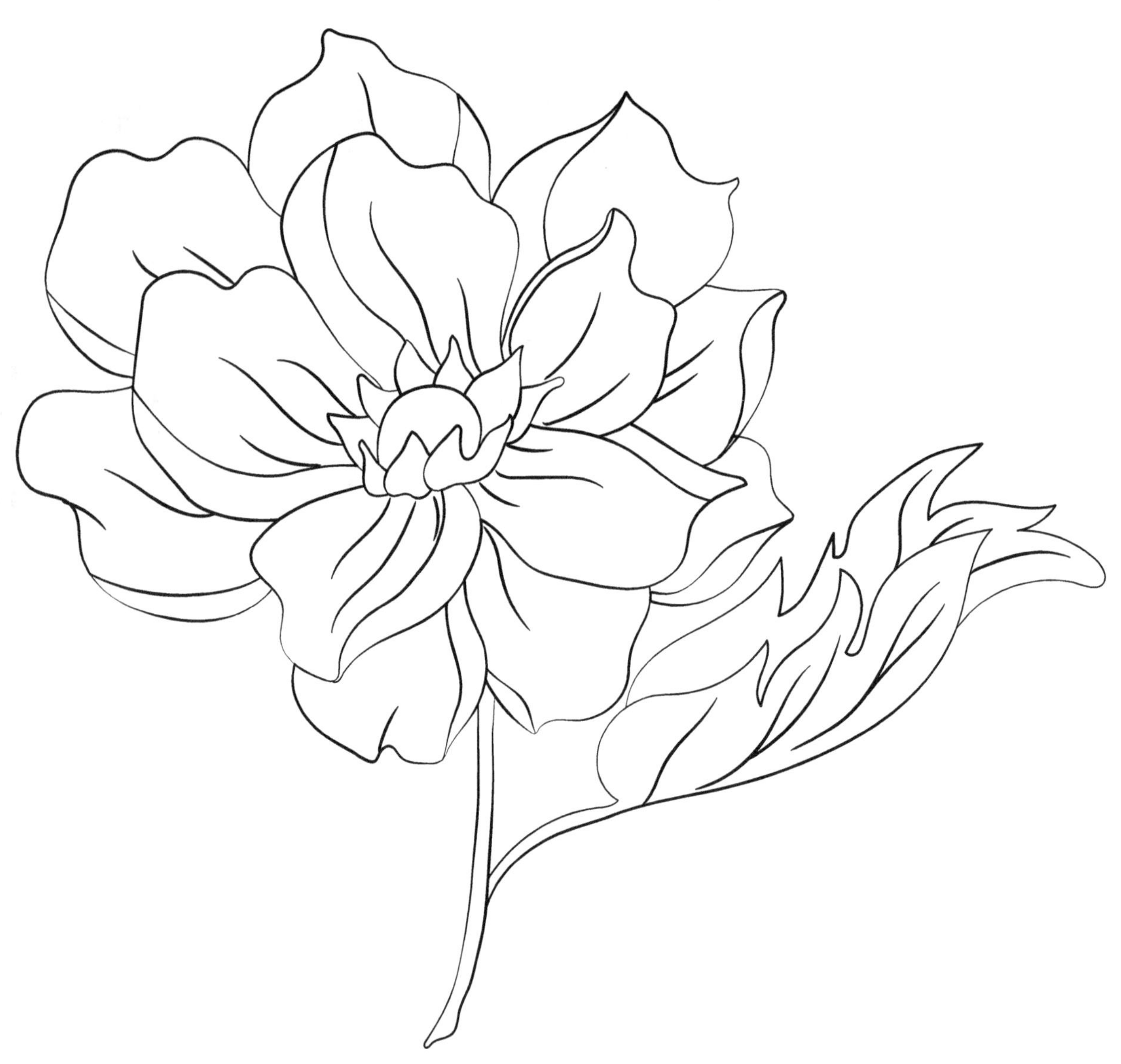

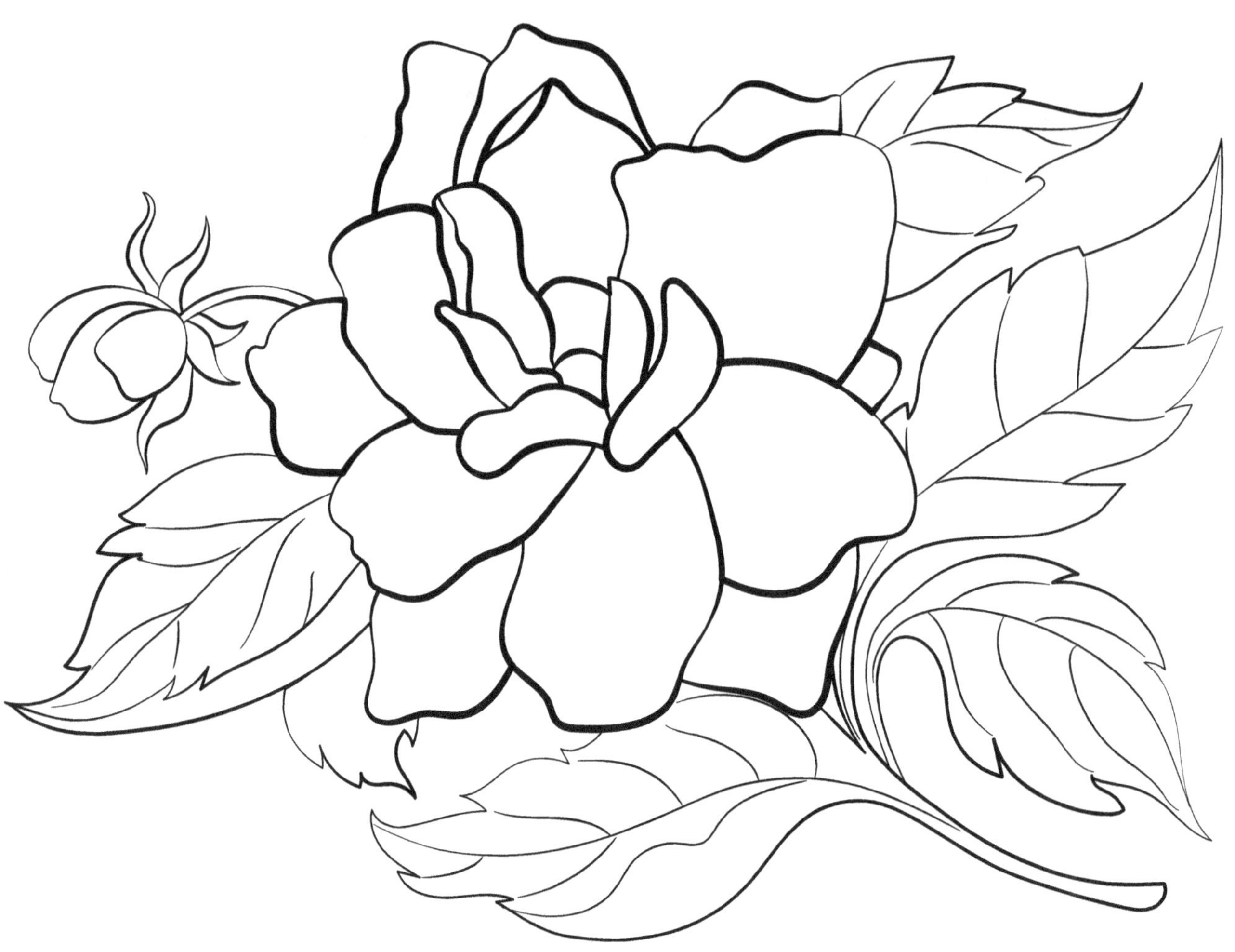

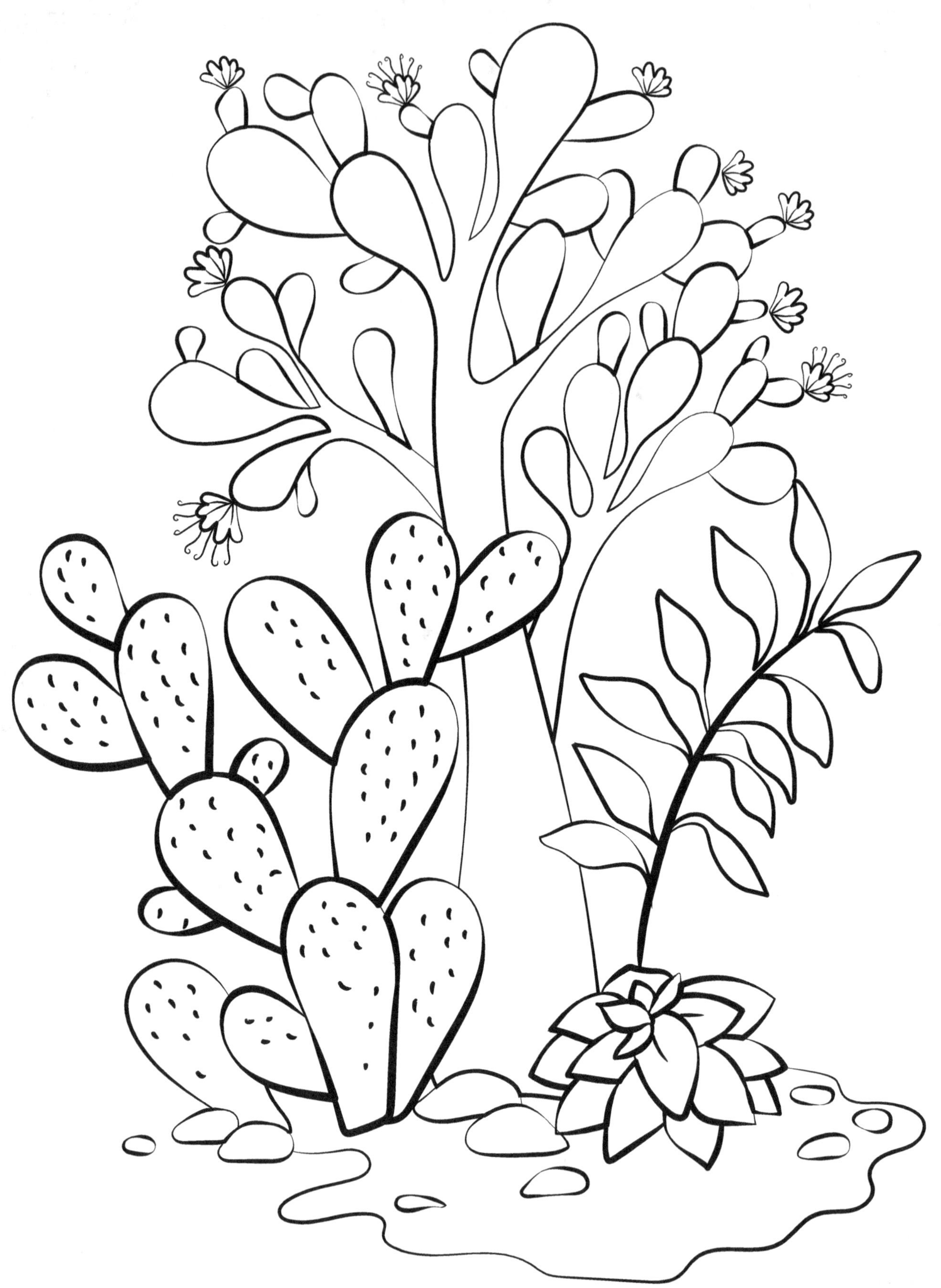

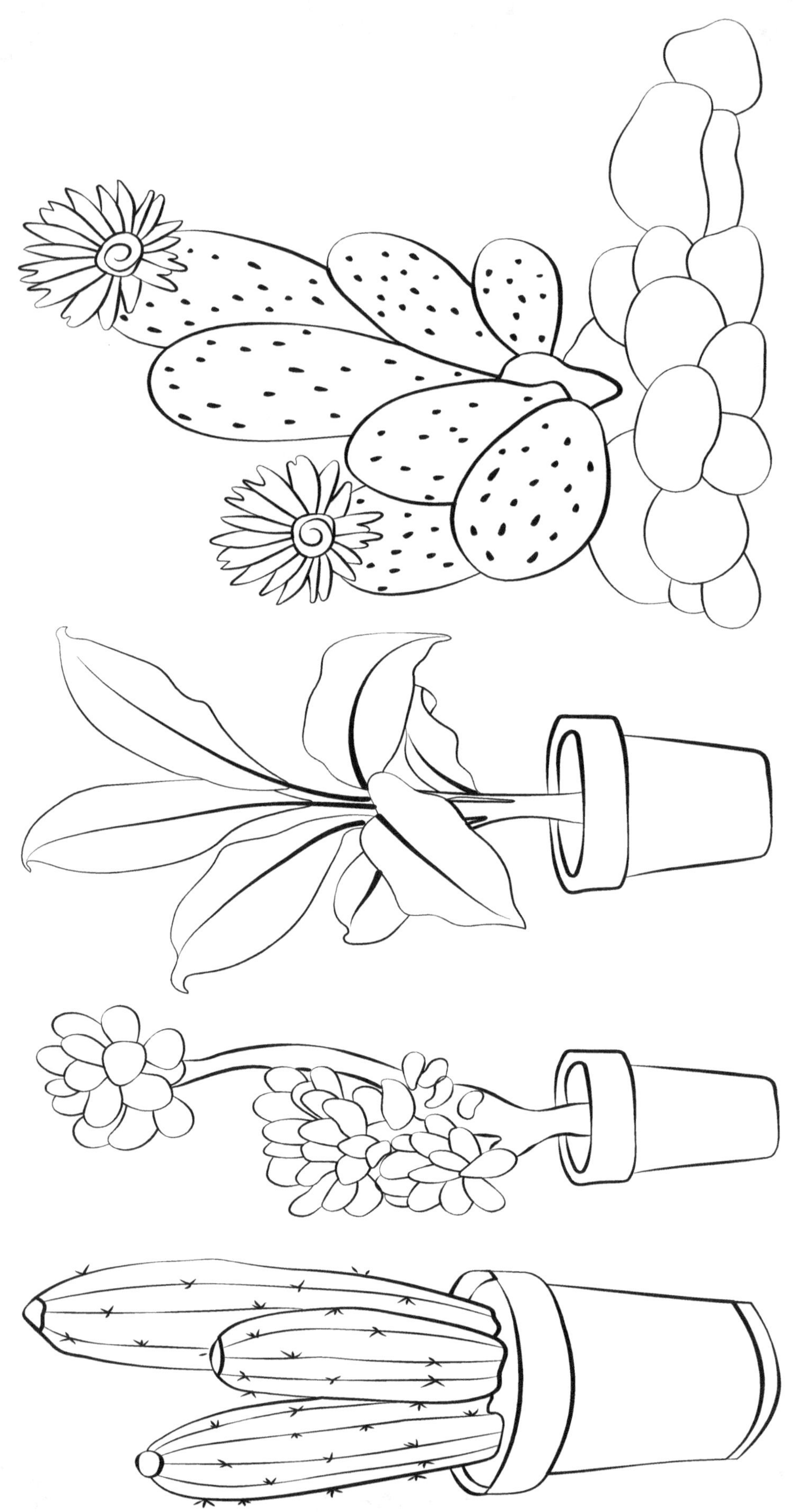

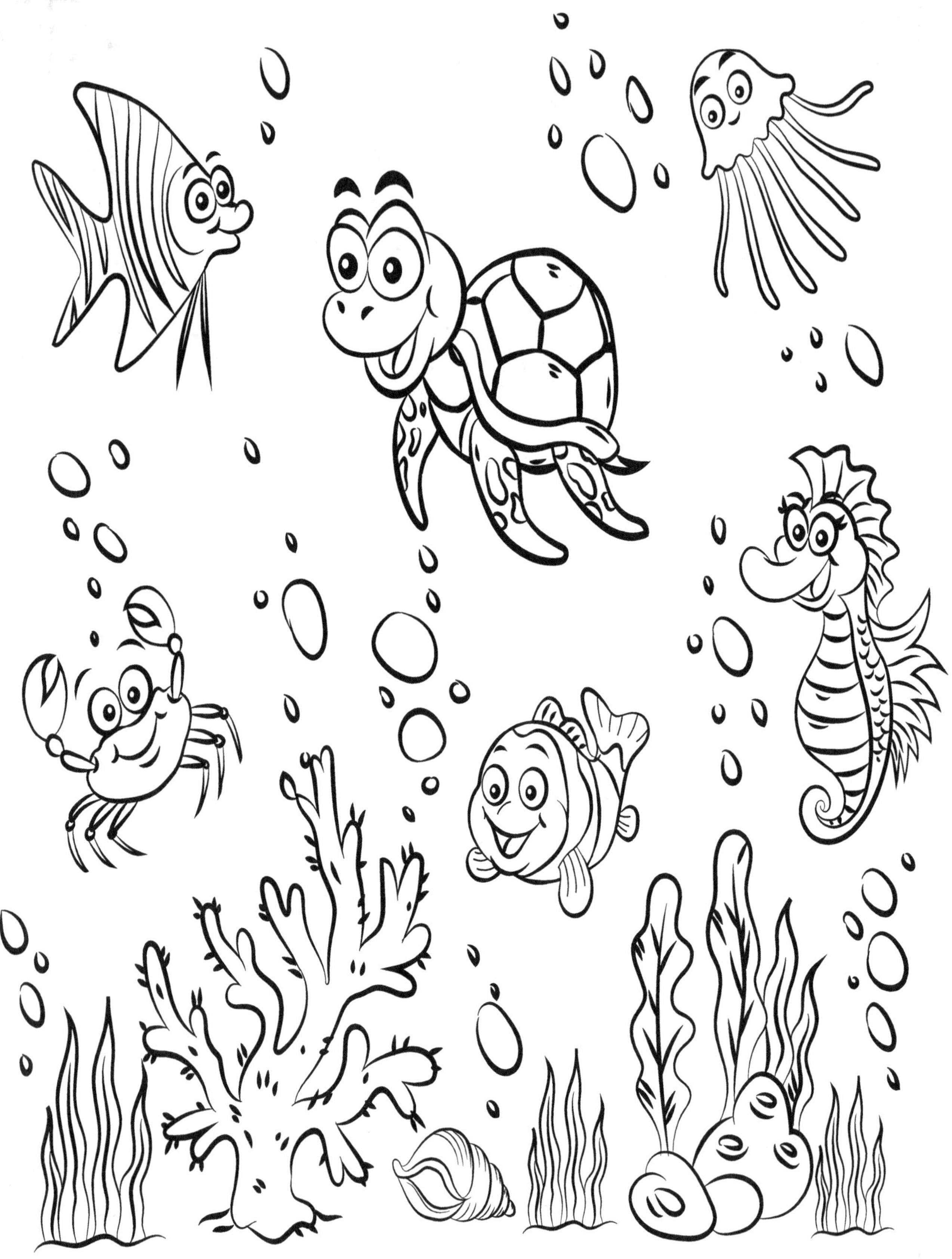

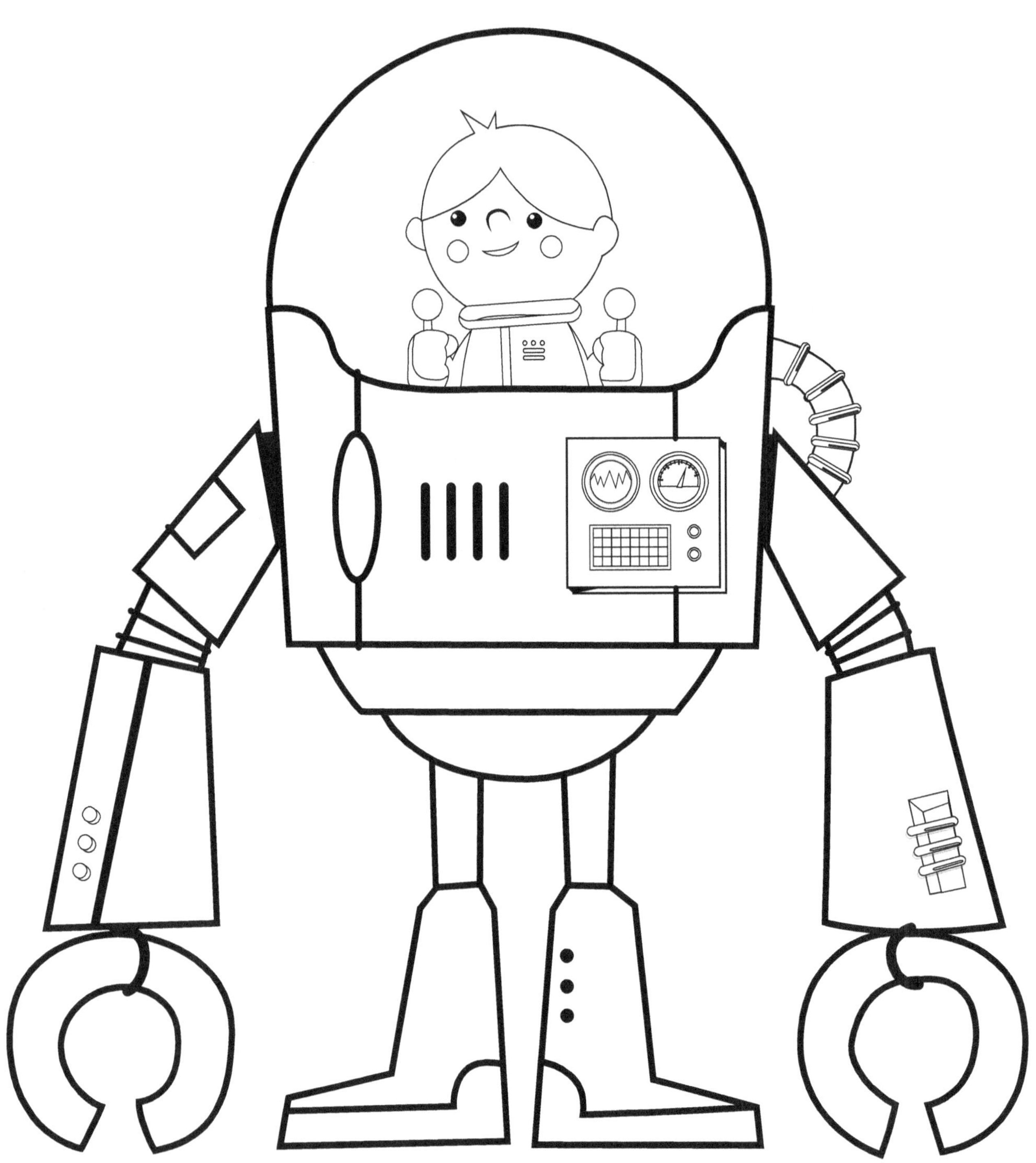

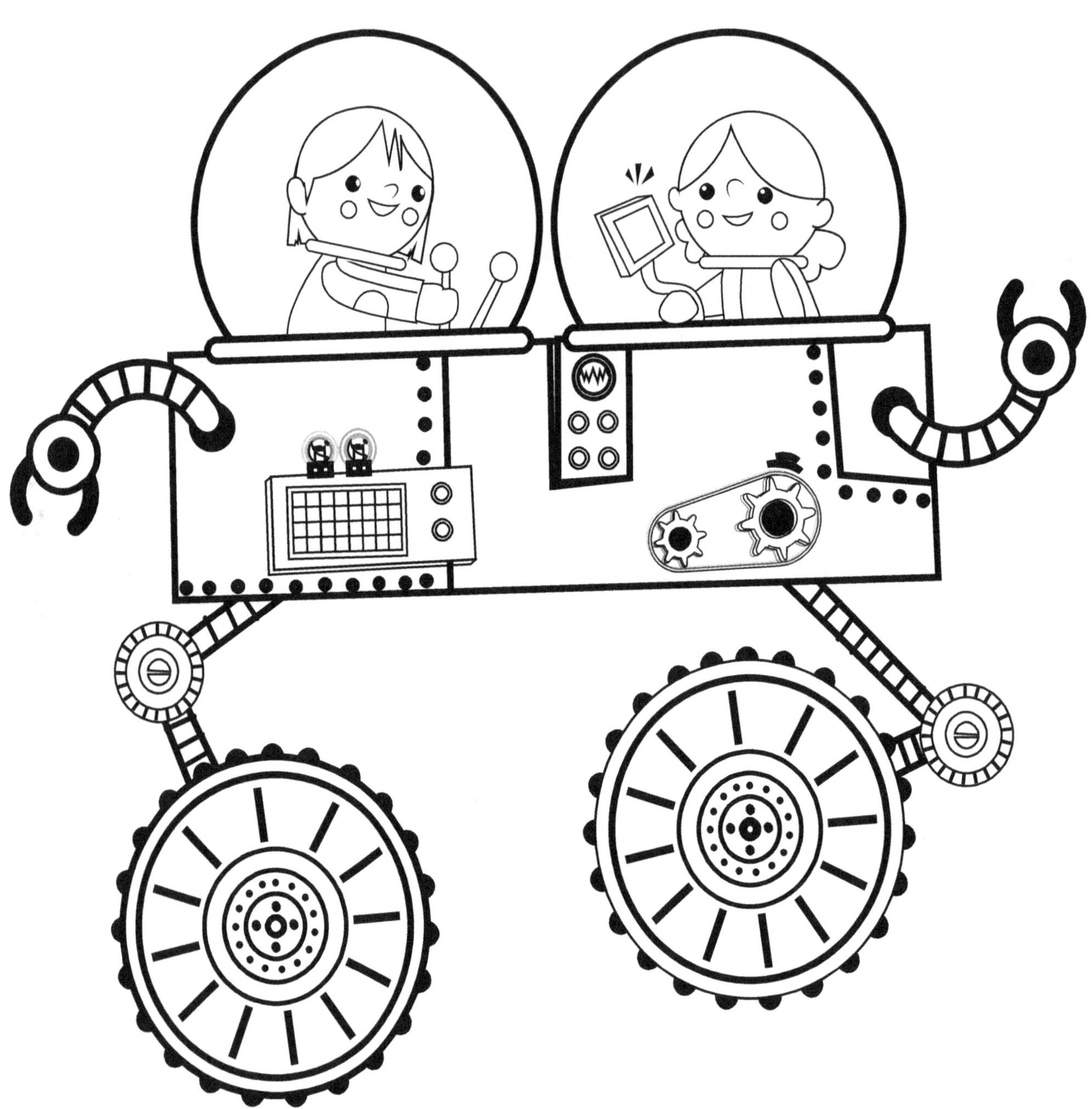

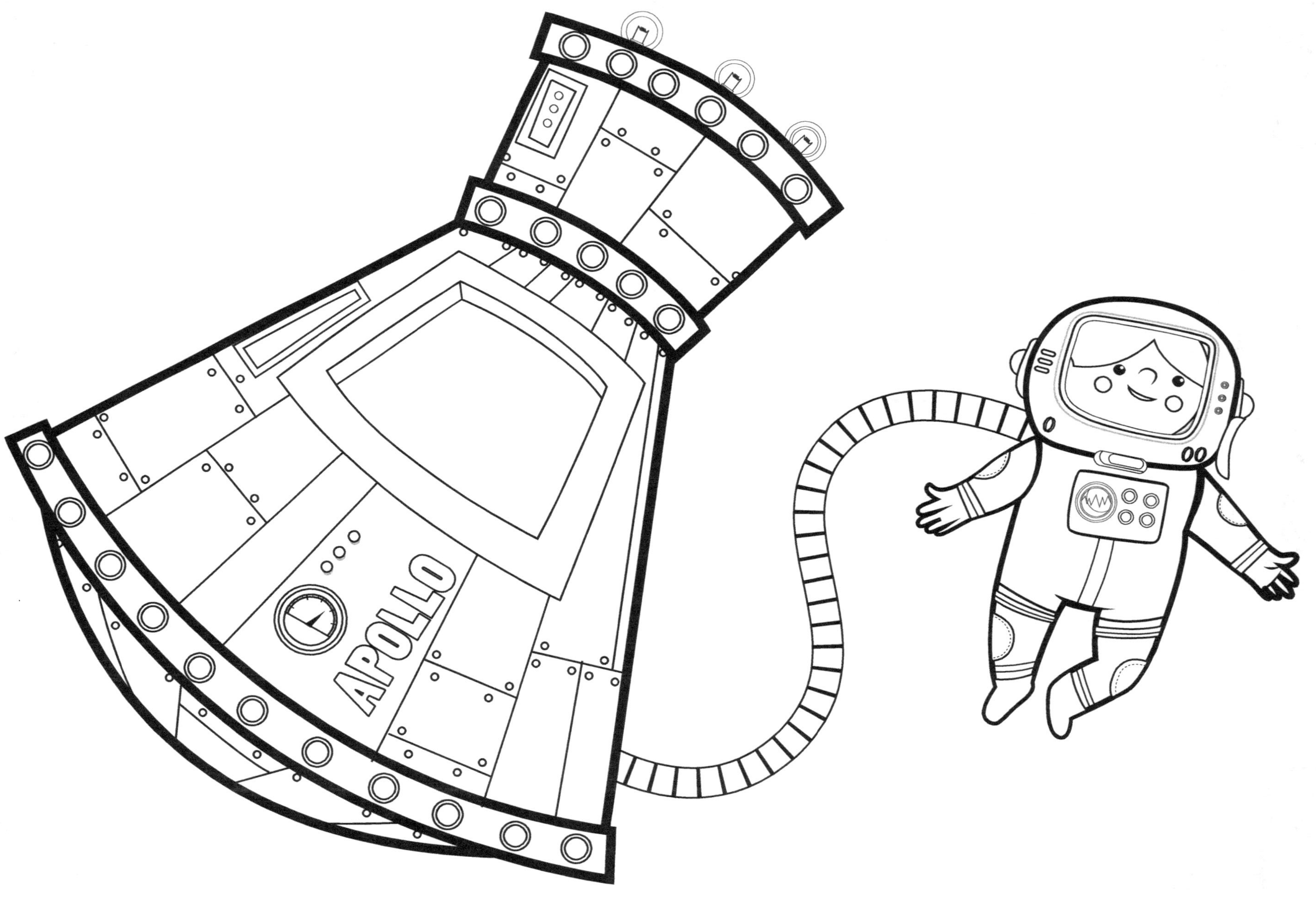

APOLLO

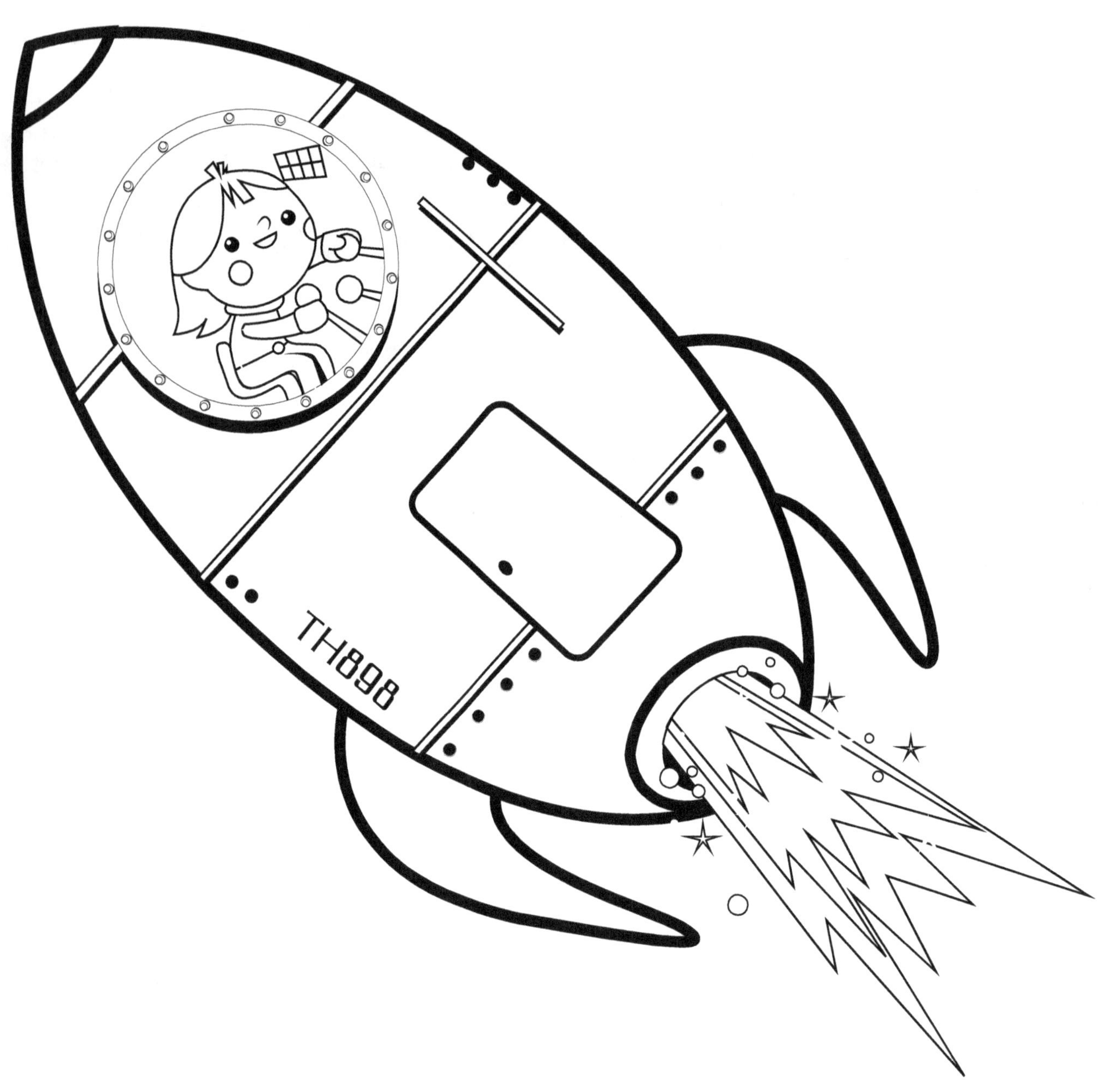

TH898

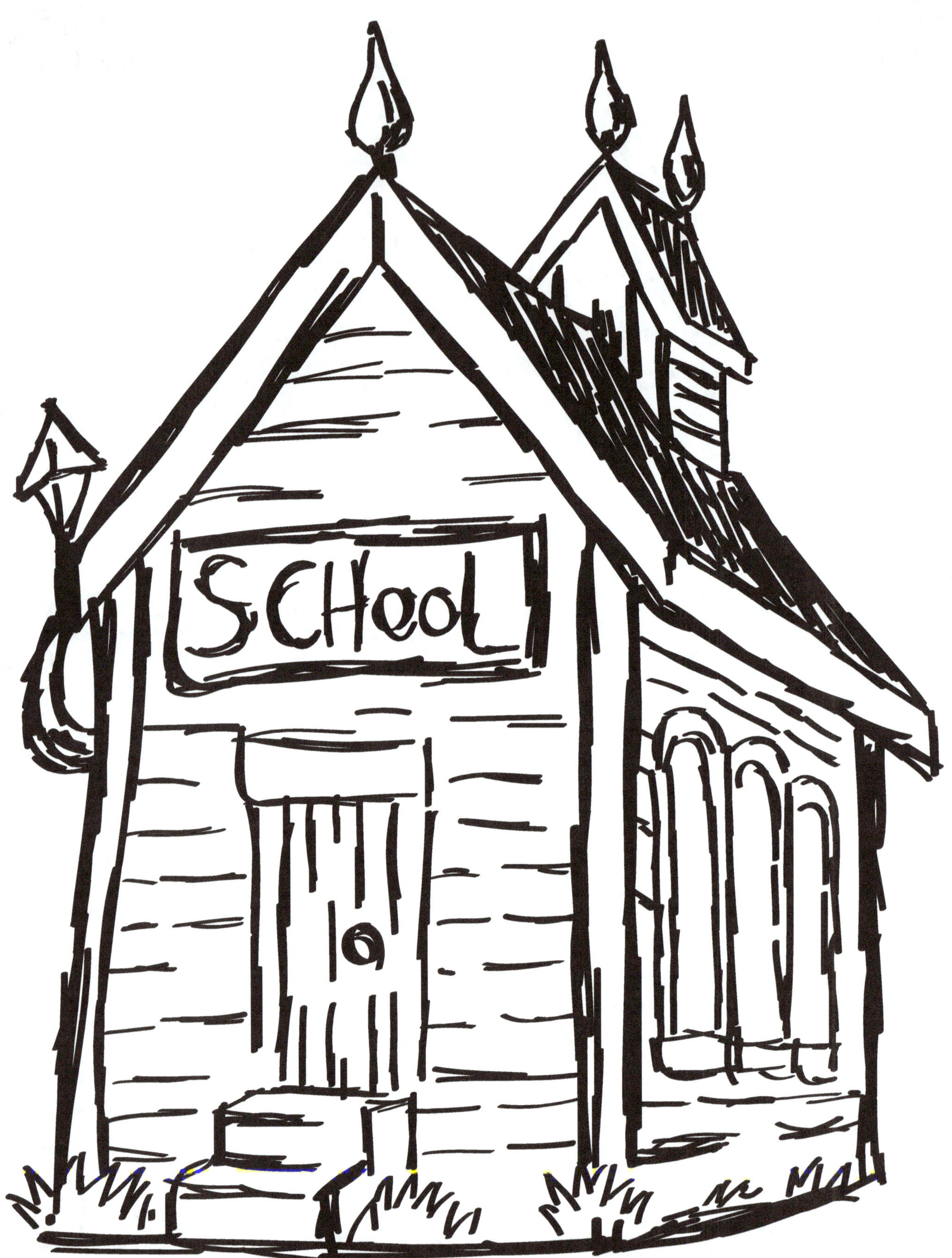

SCHOOL

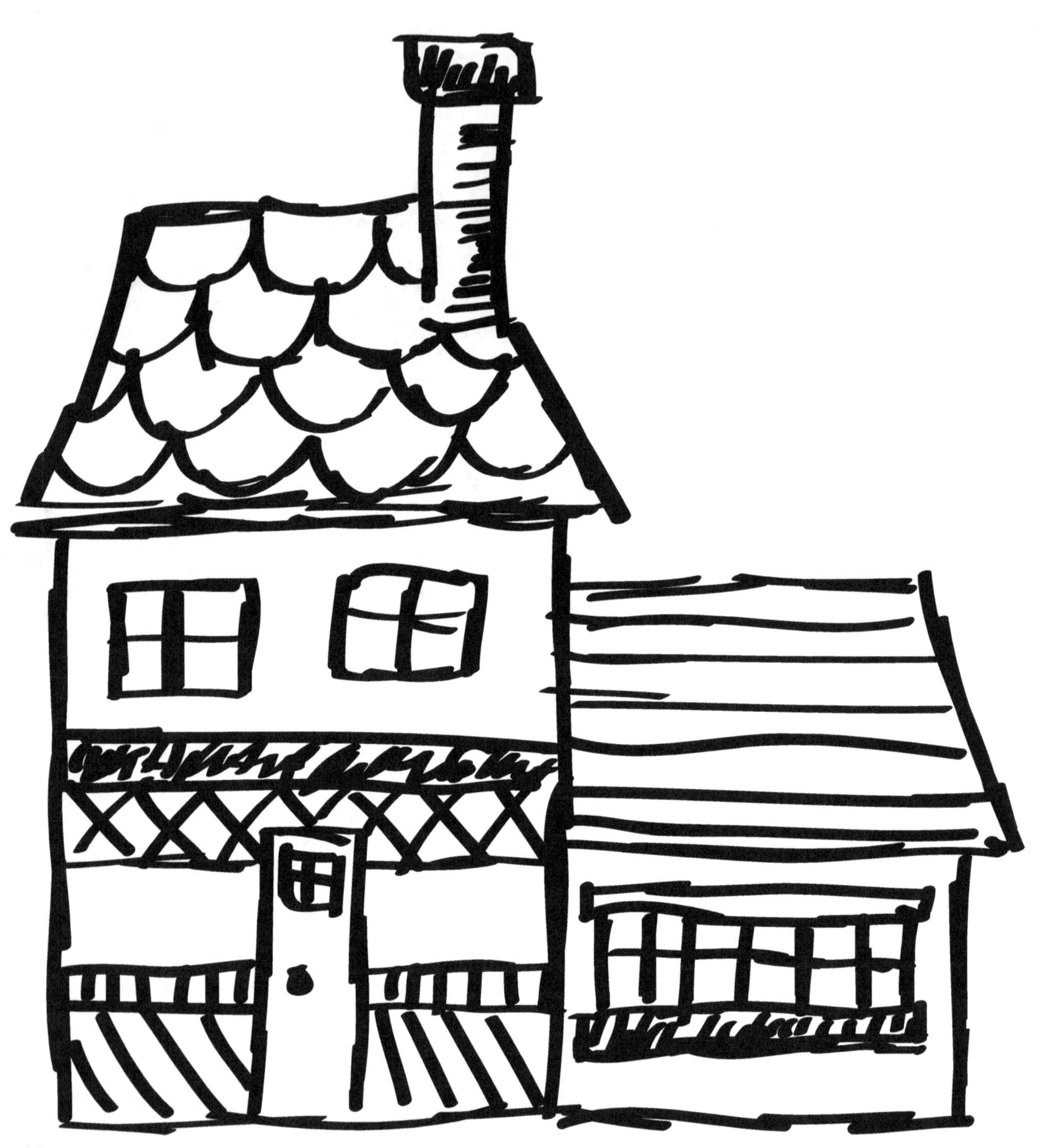

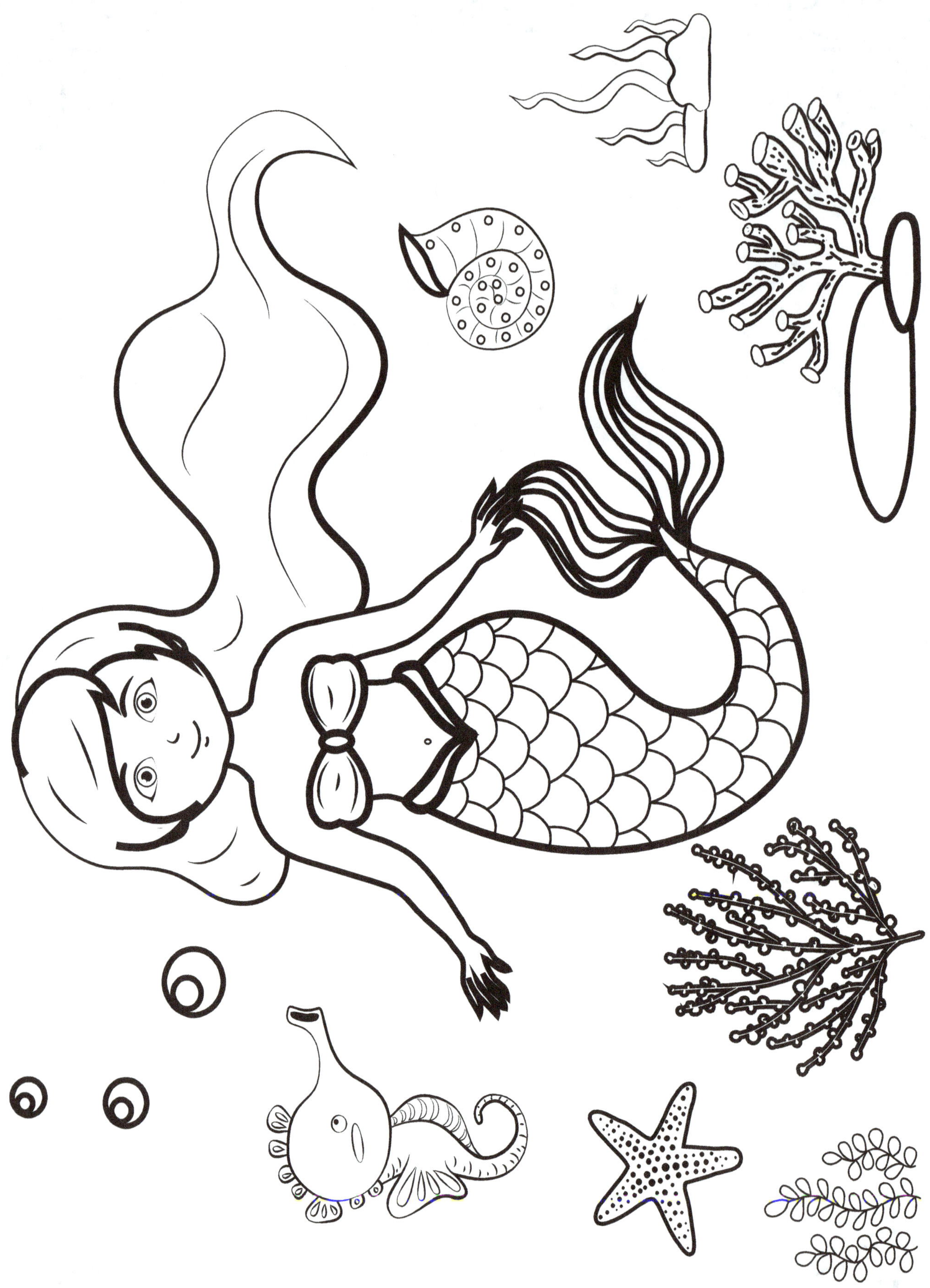

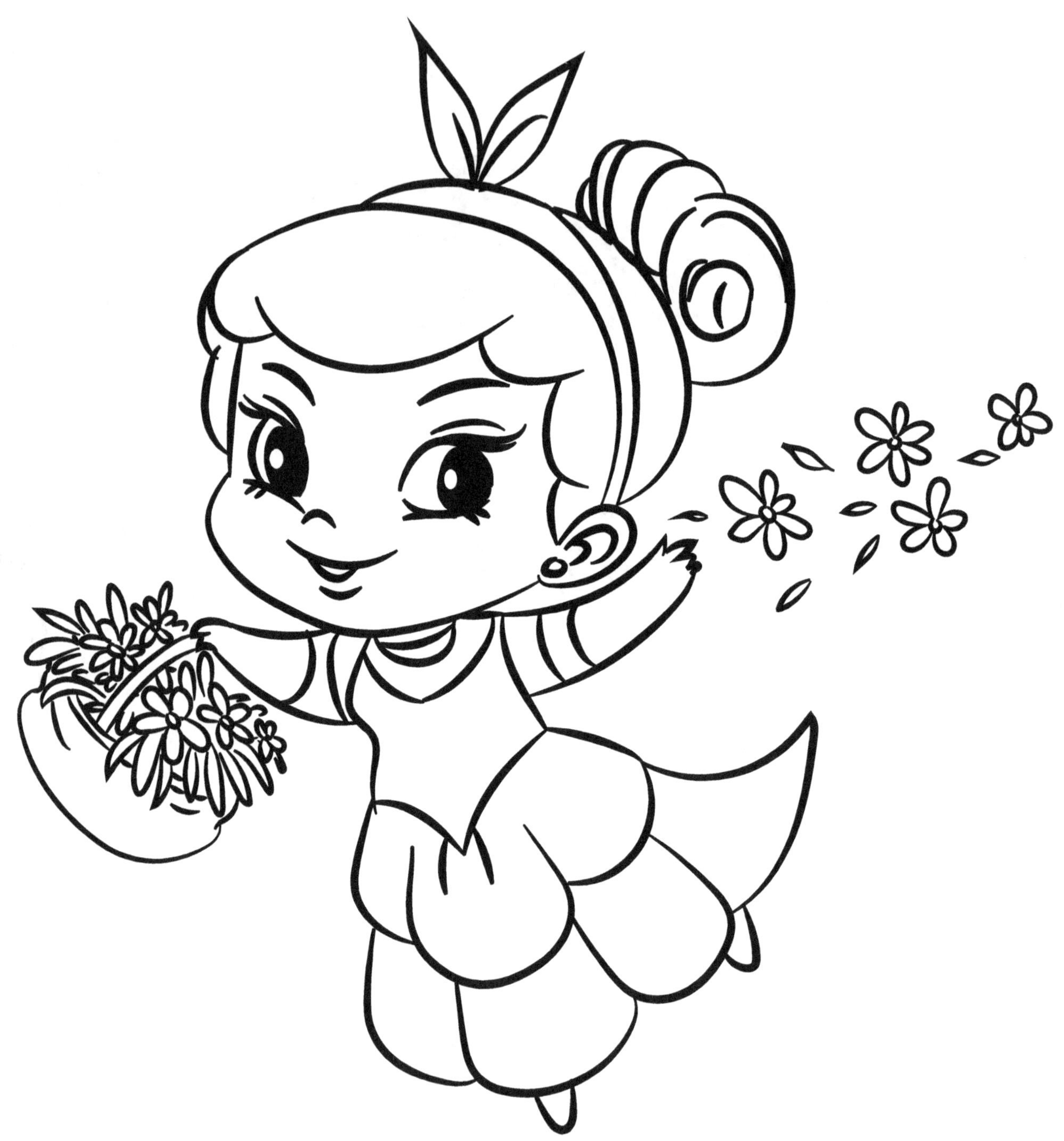

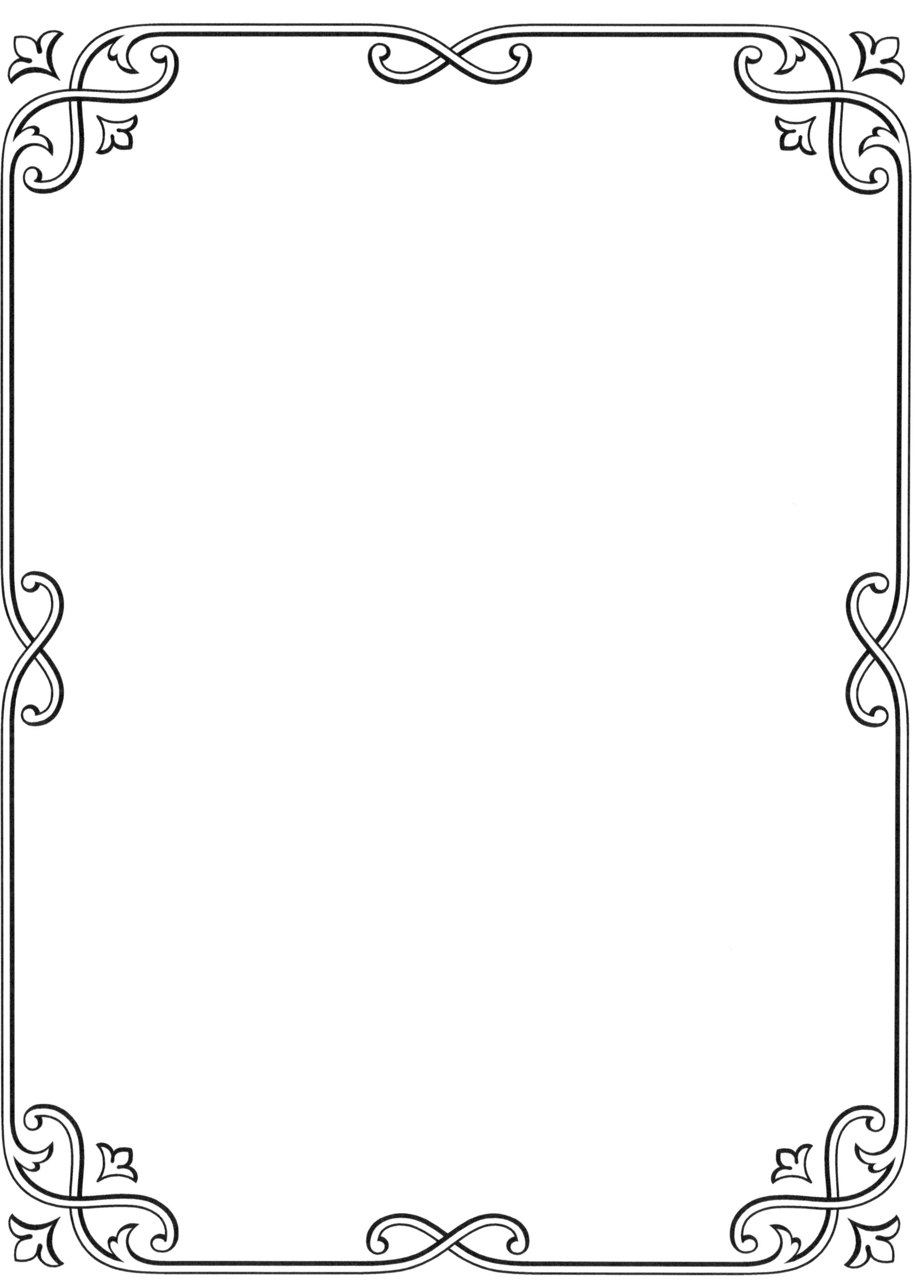

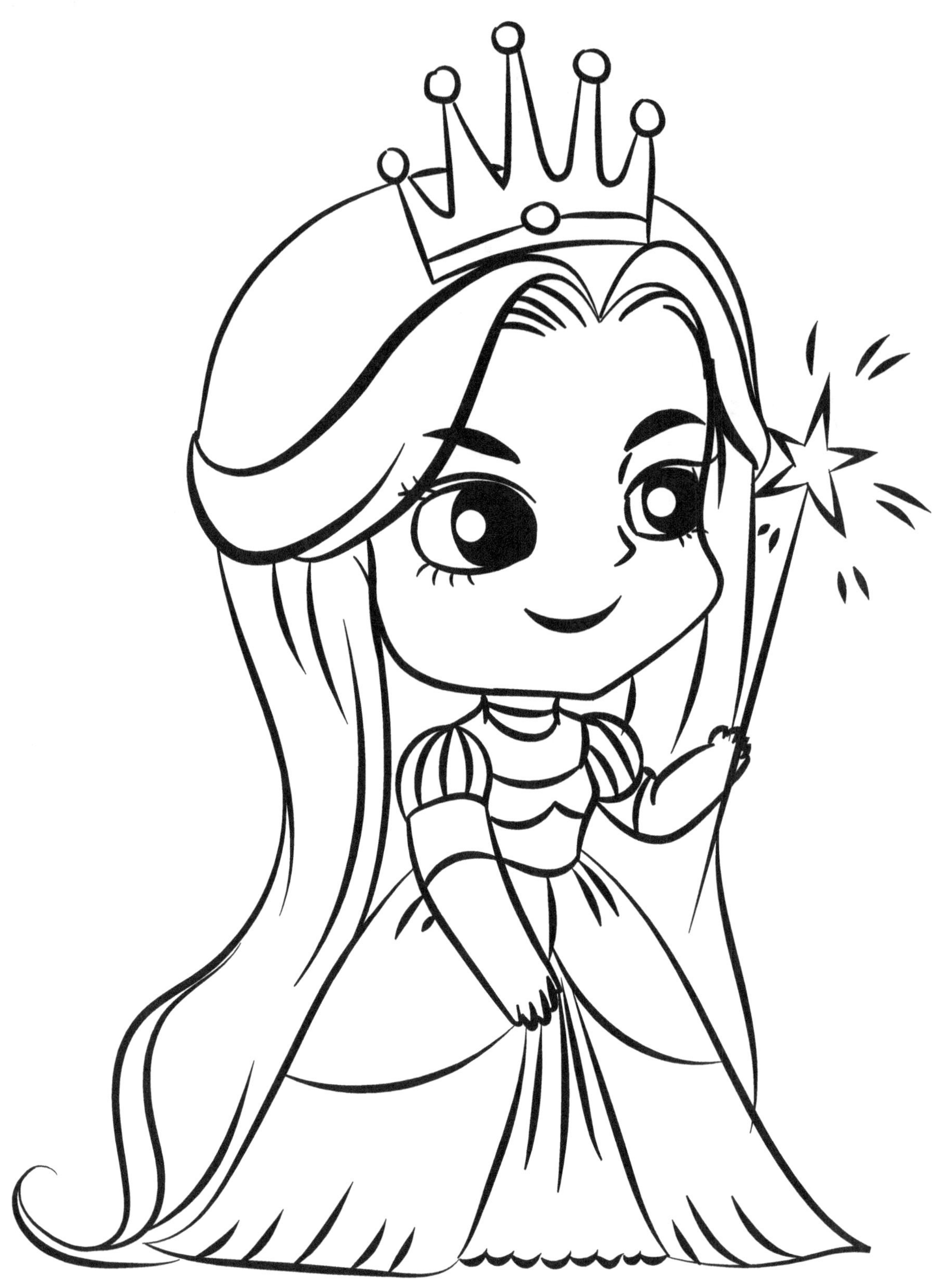

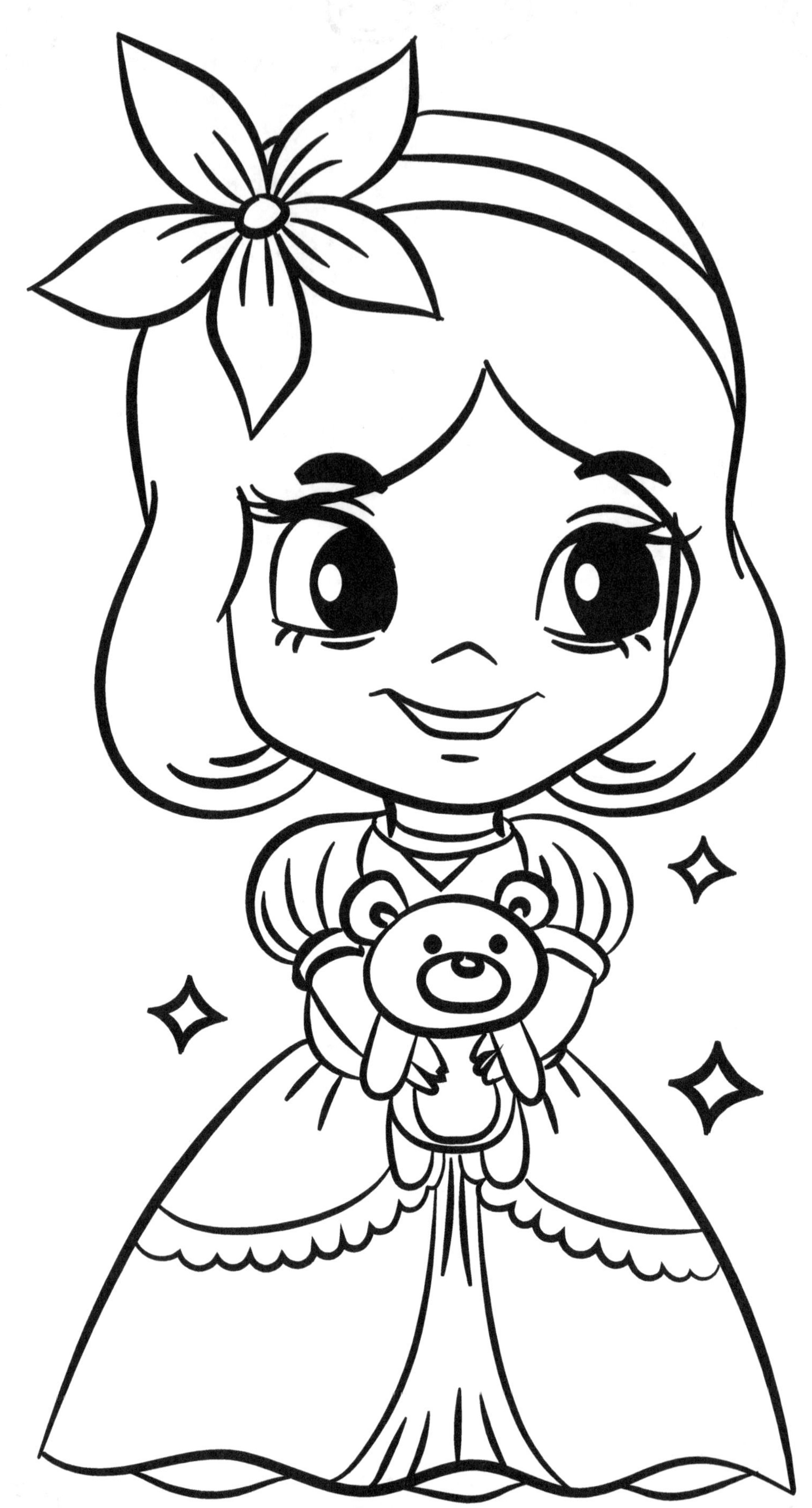

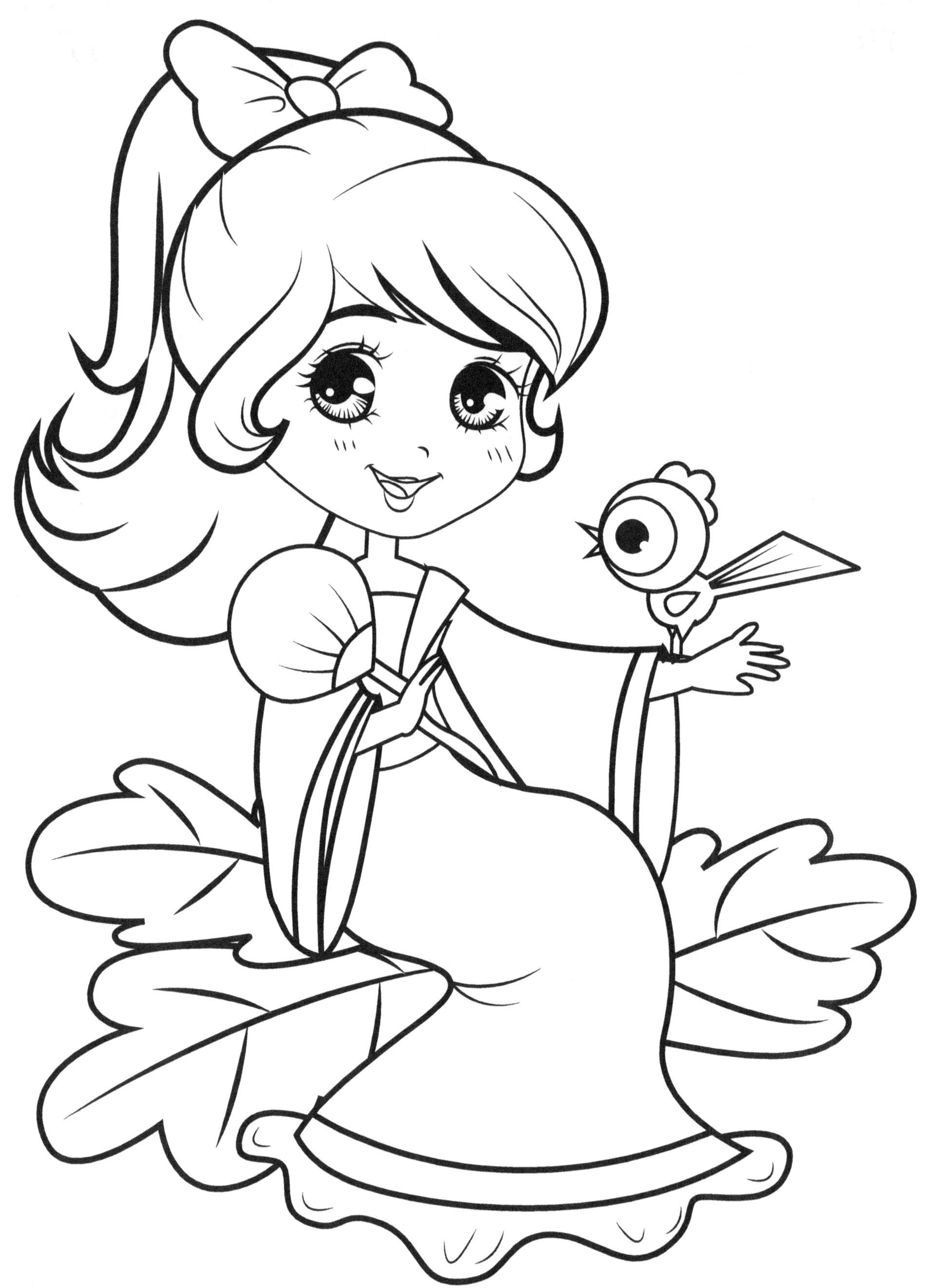

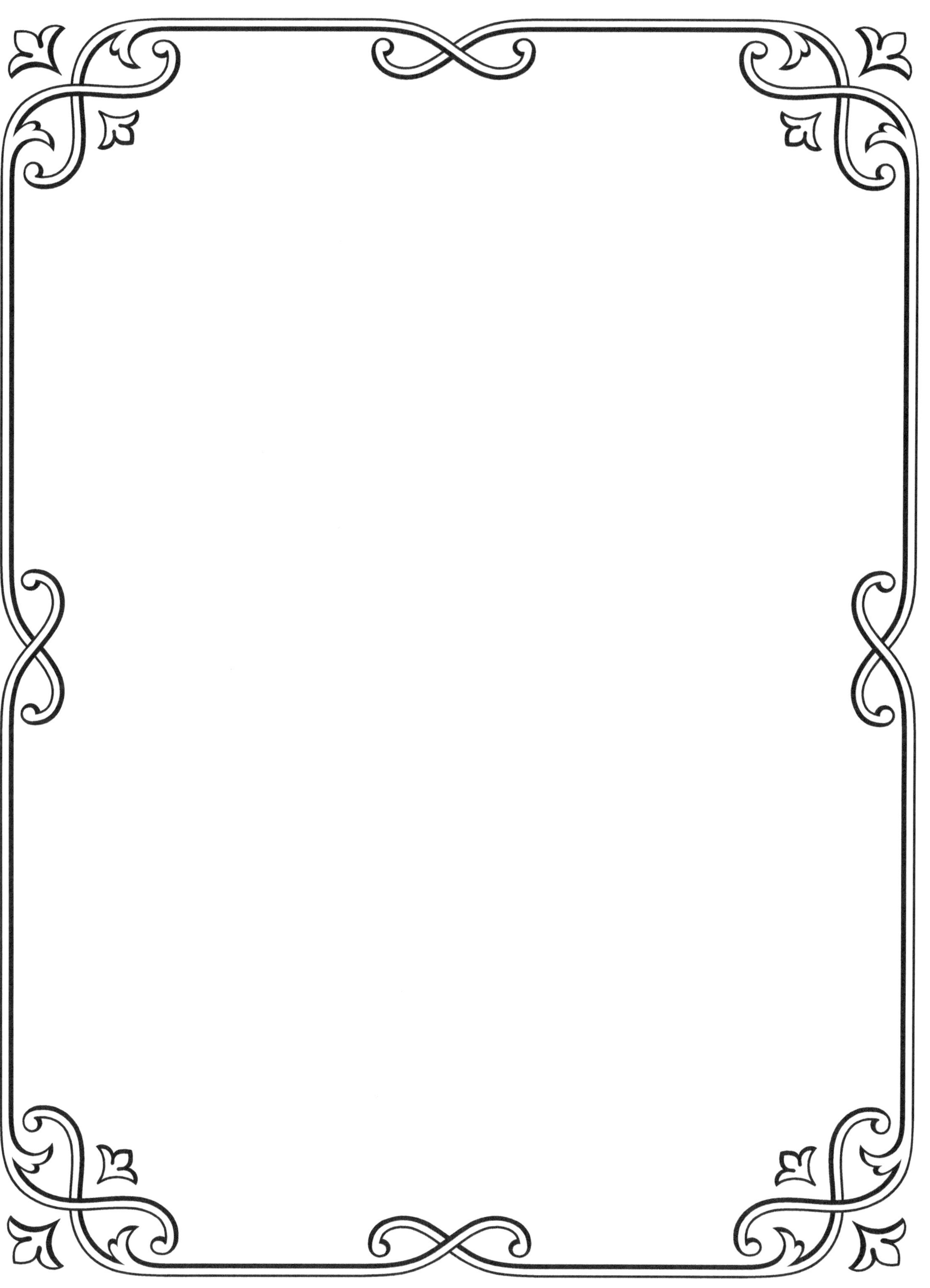

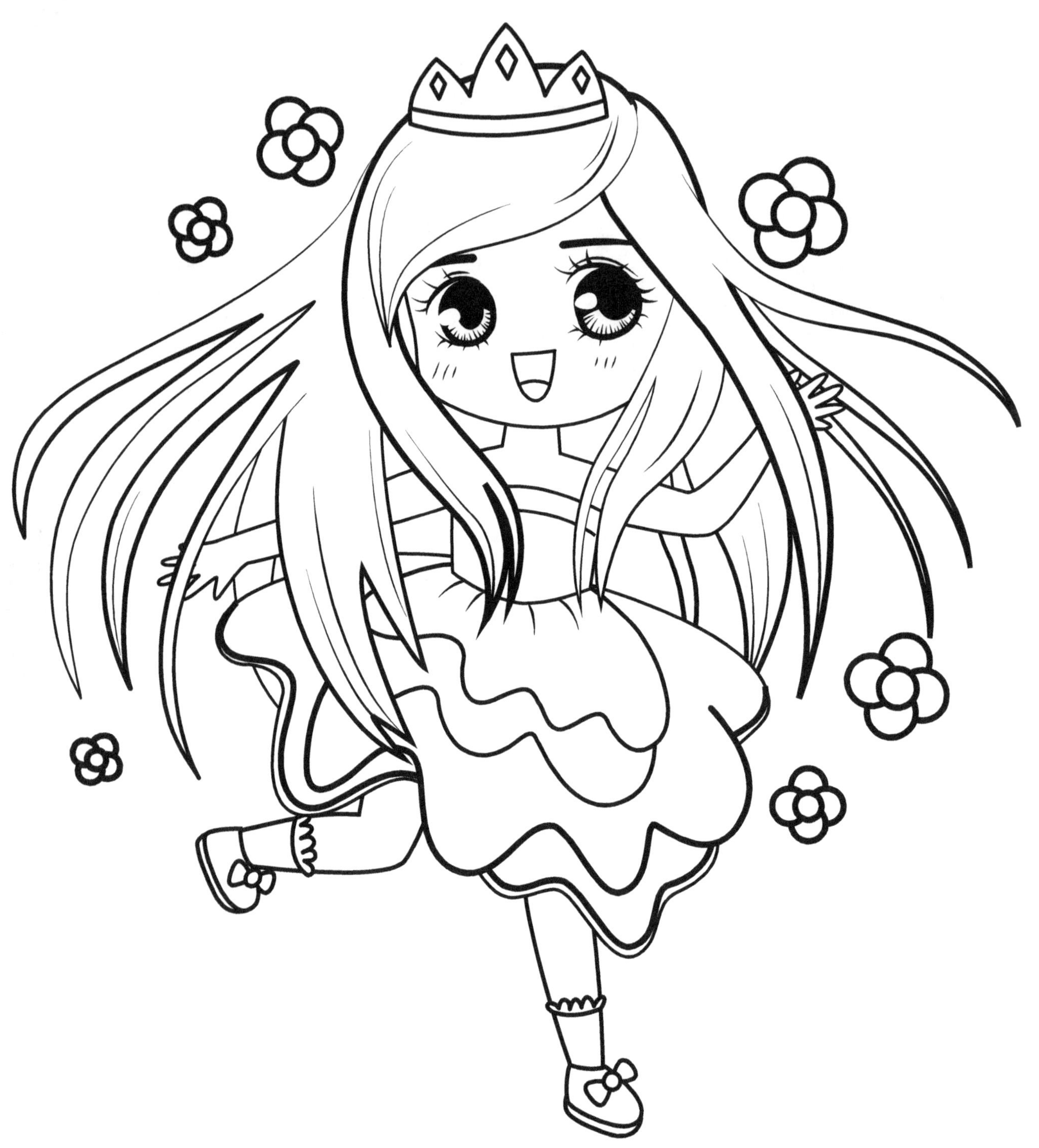

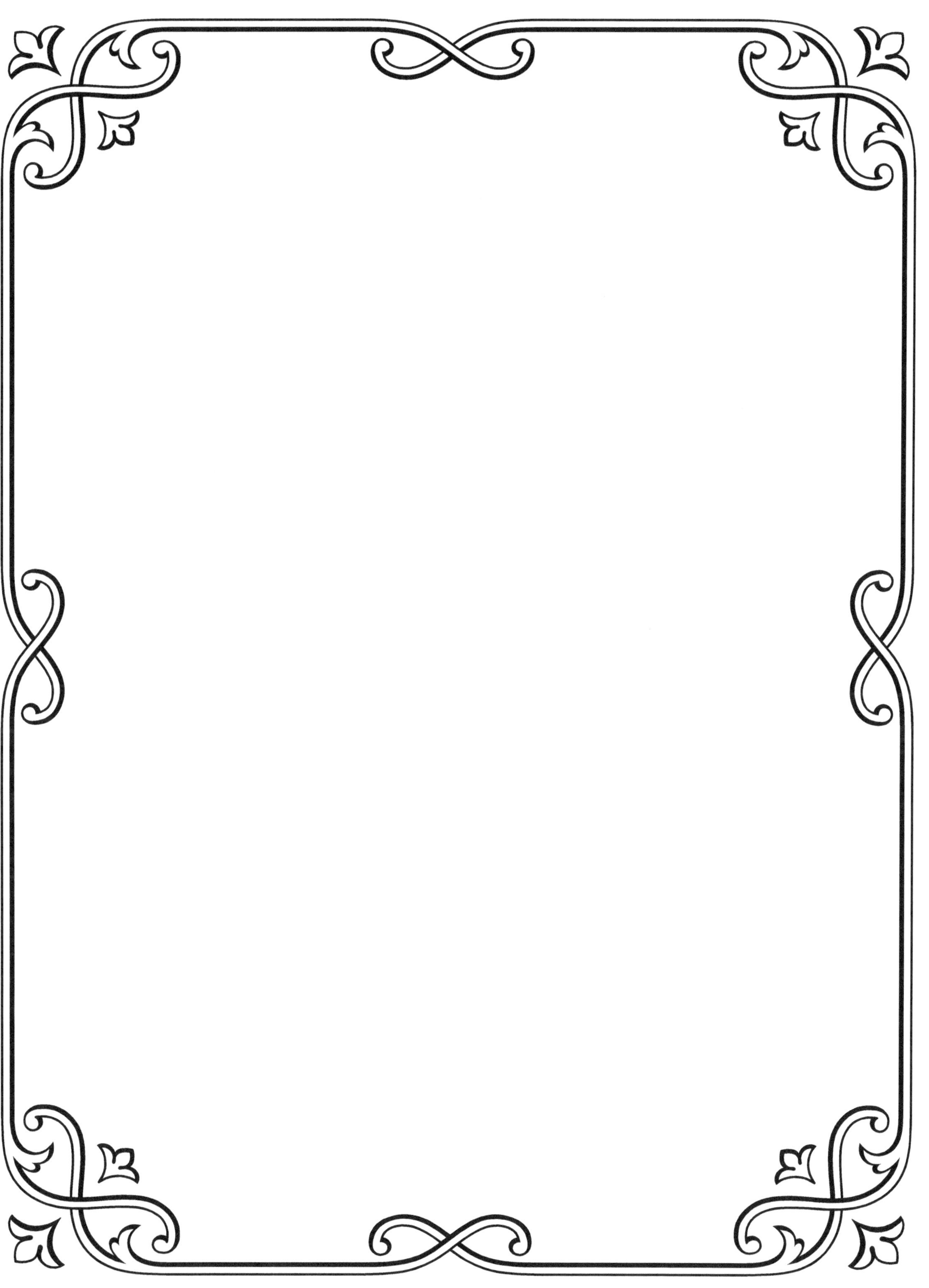

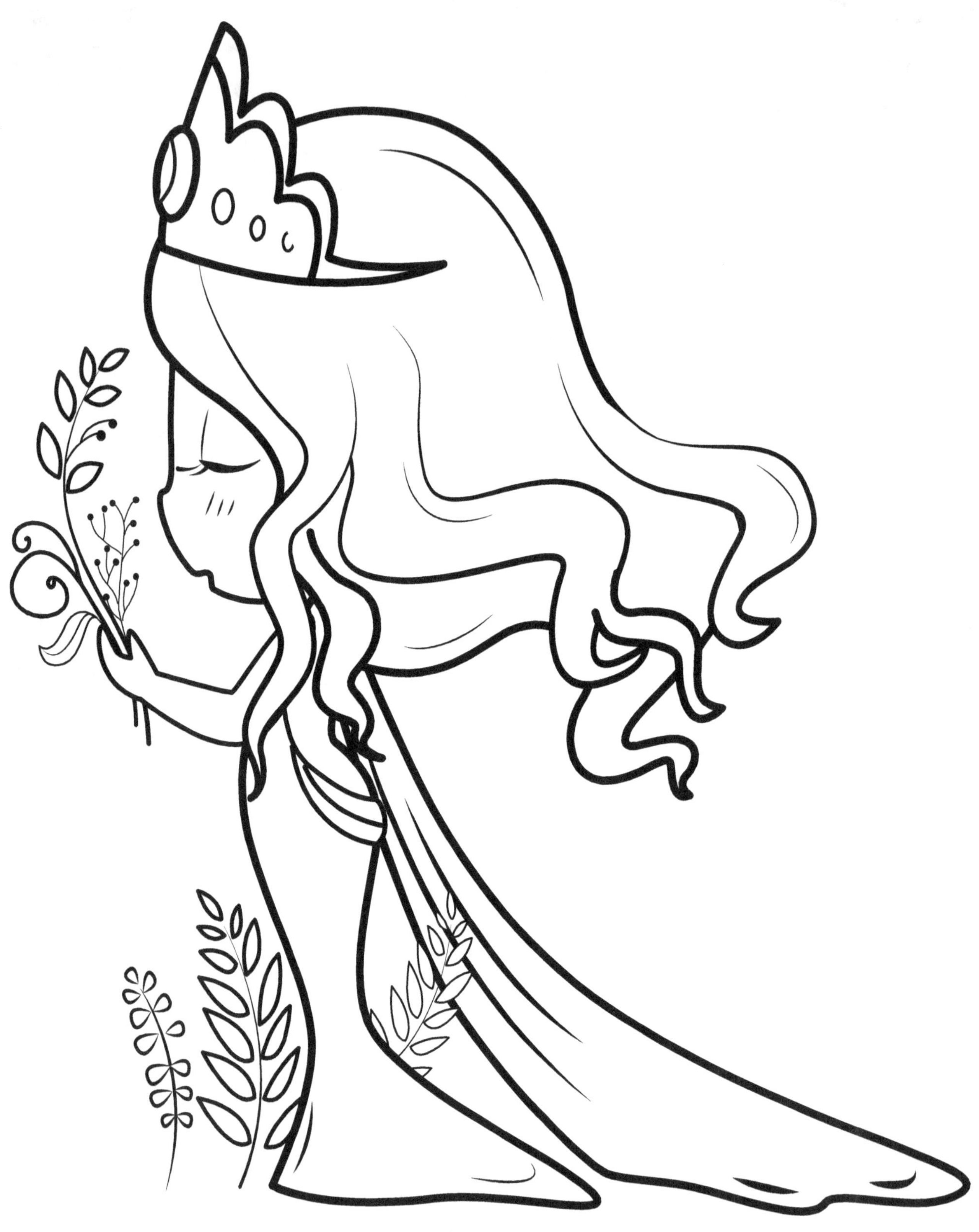

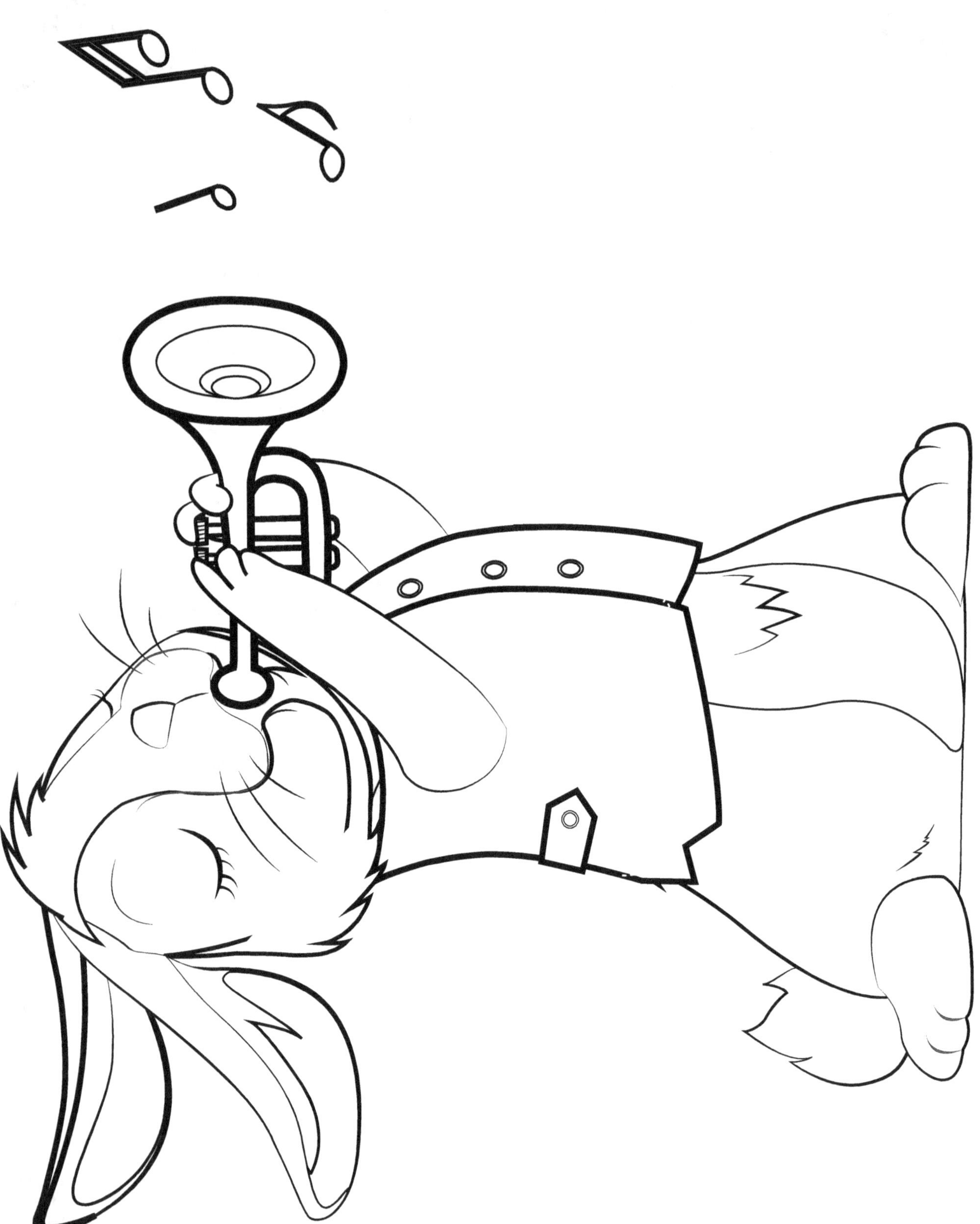

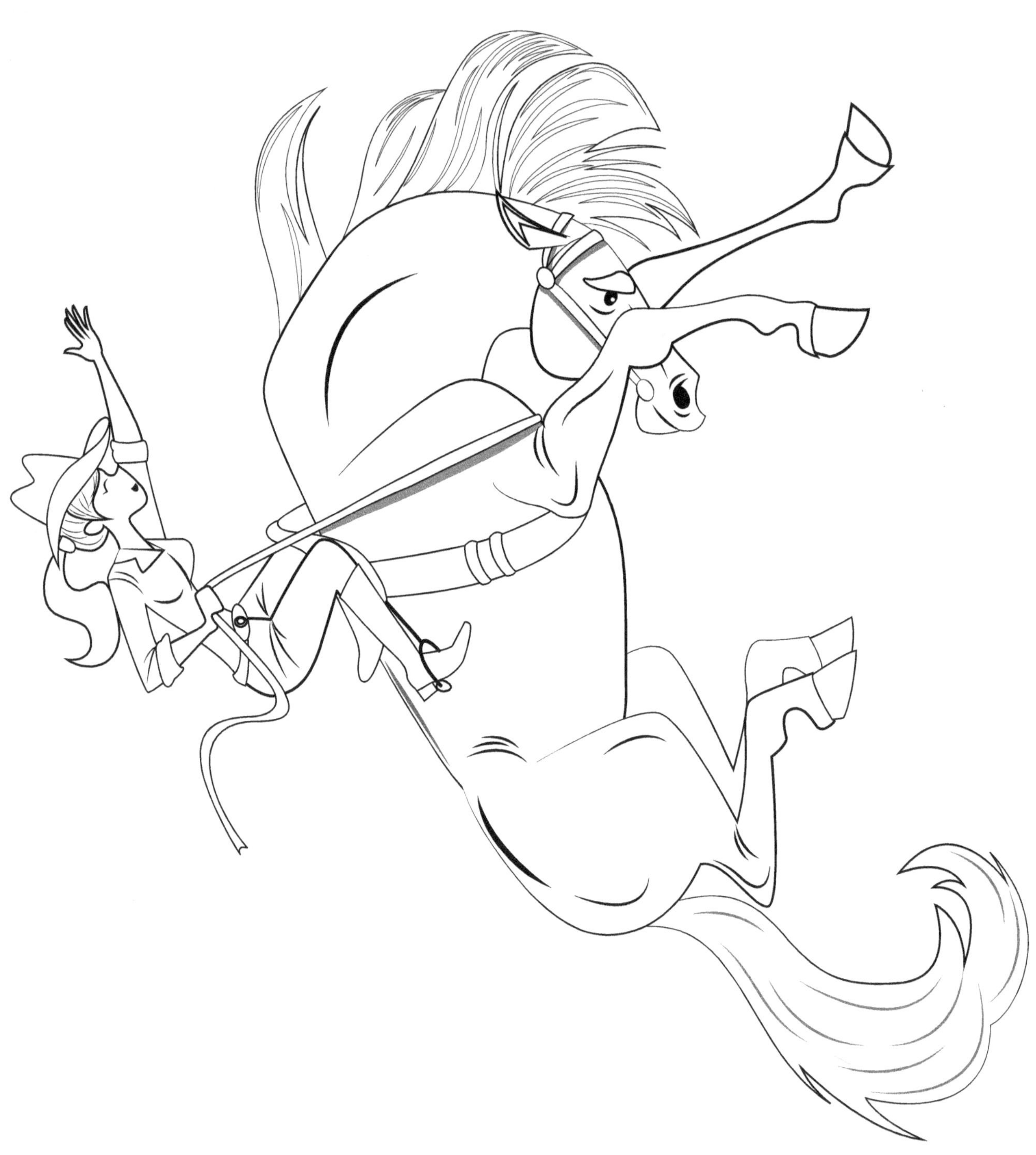

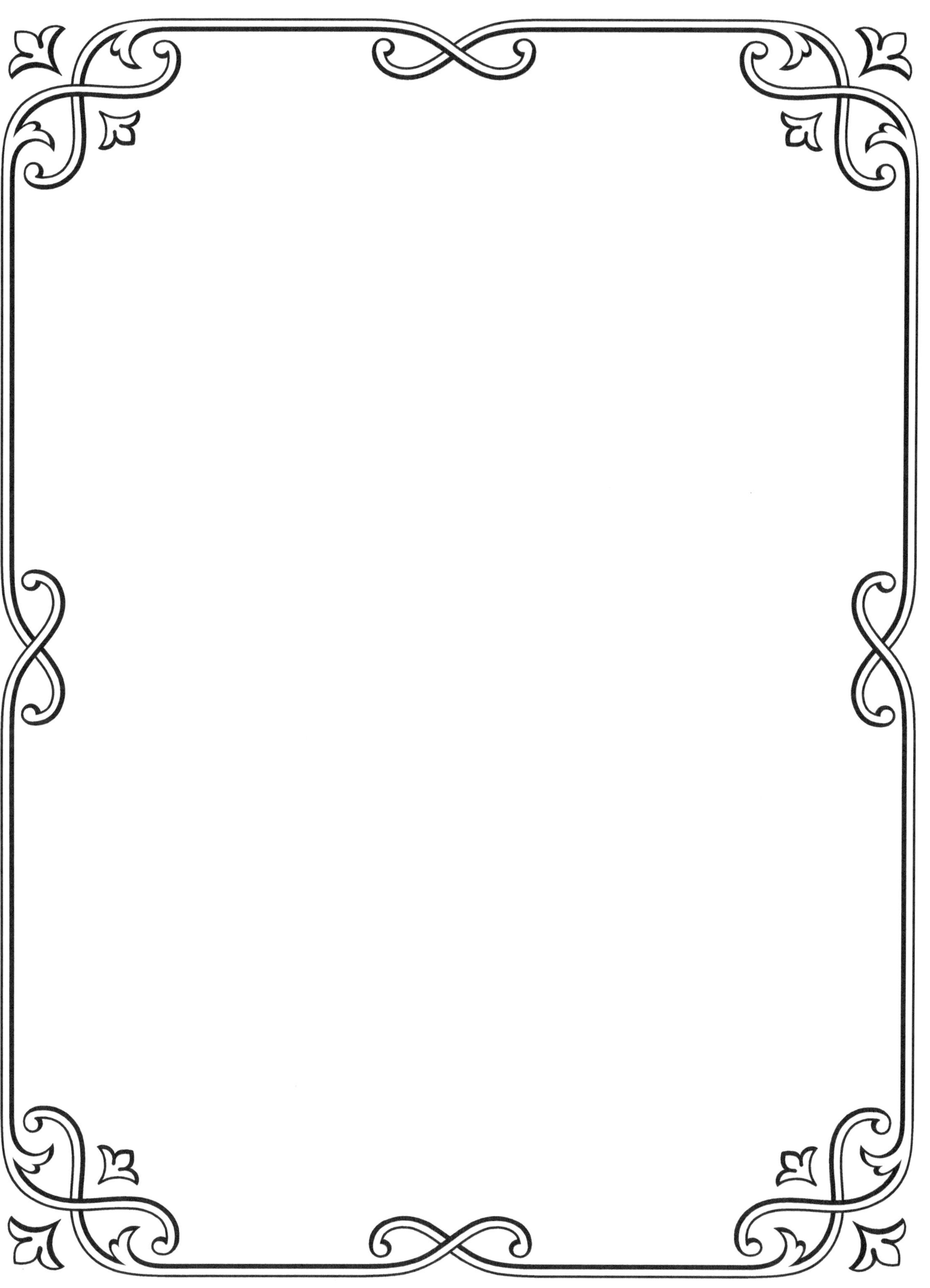

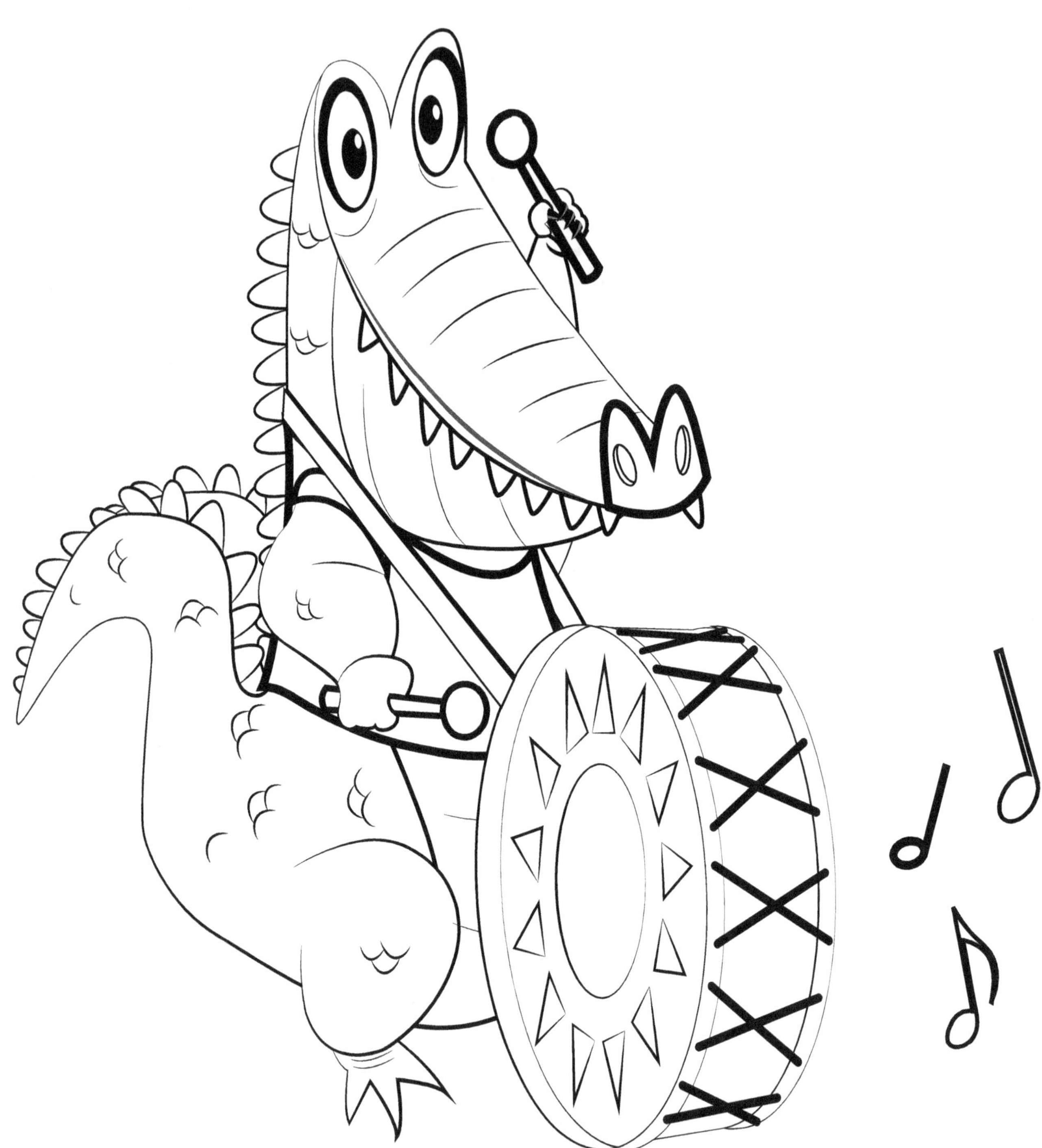

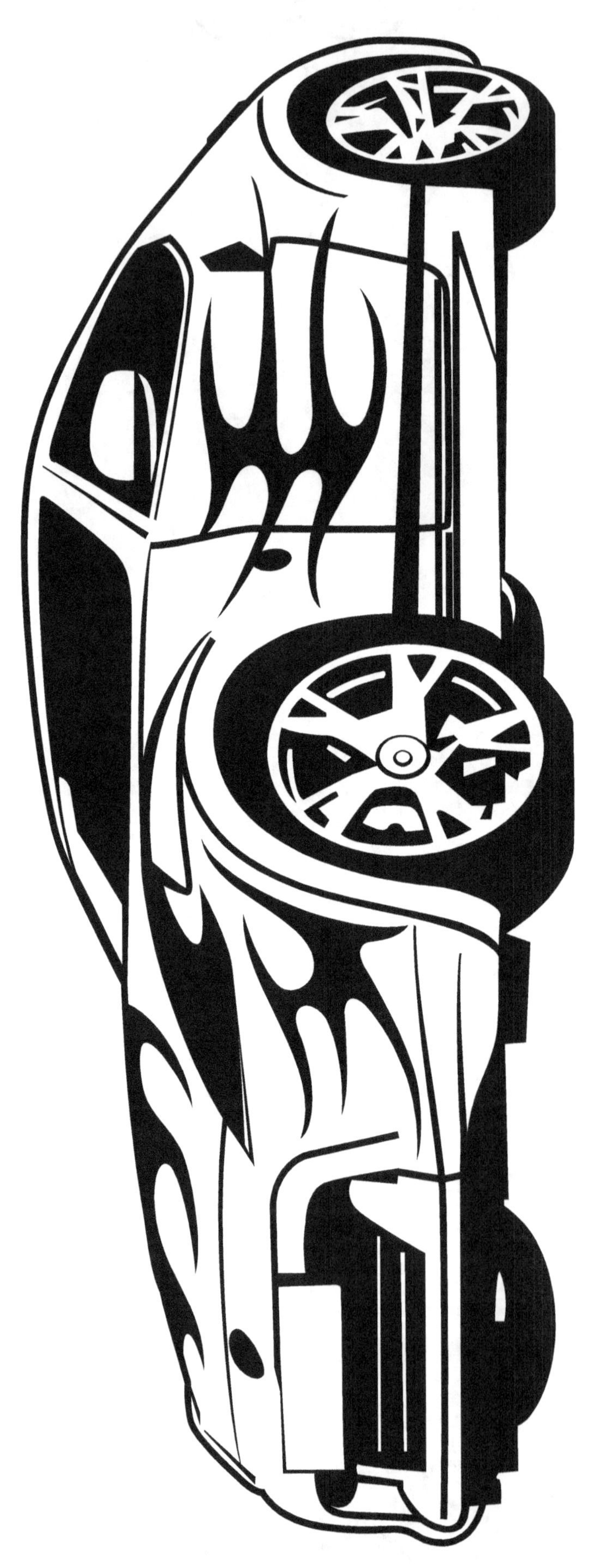

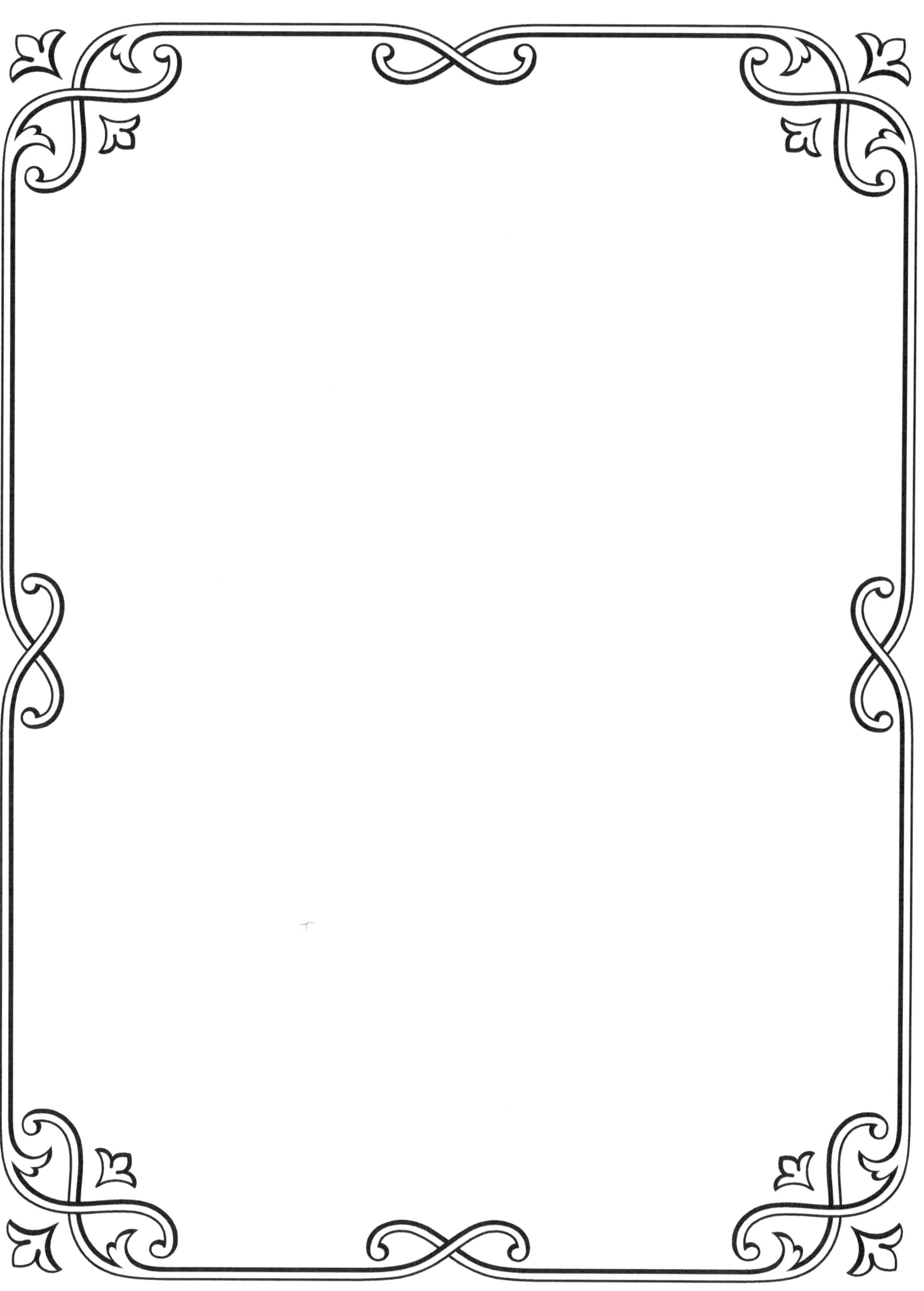

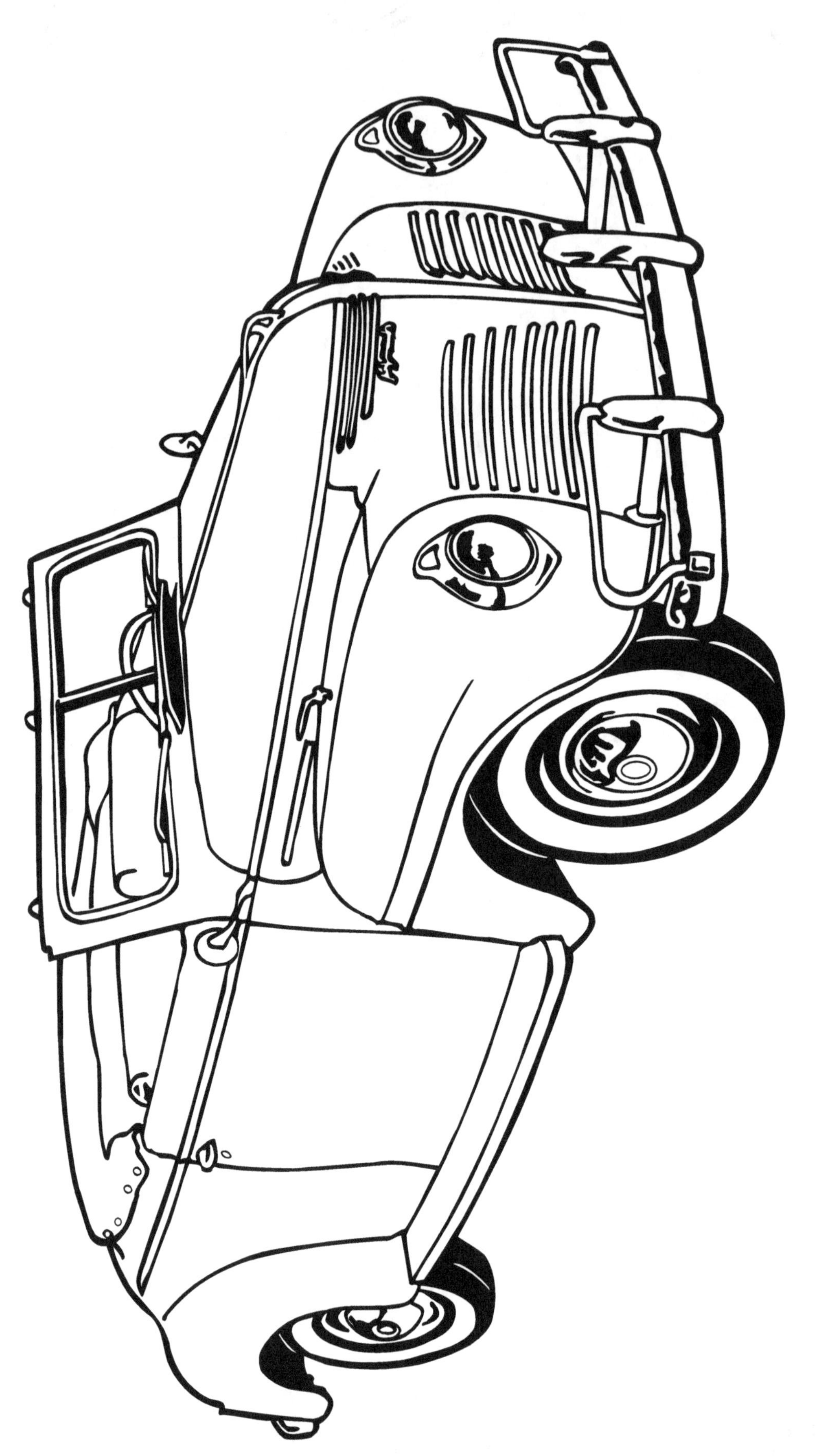

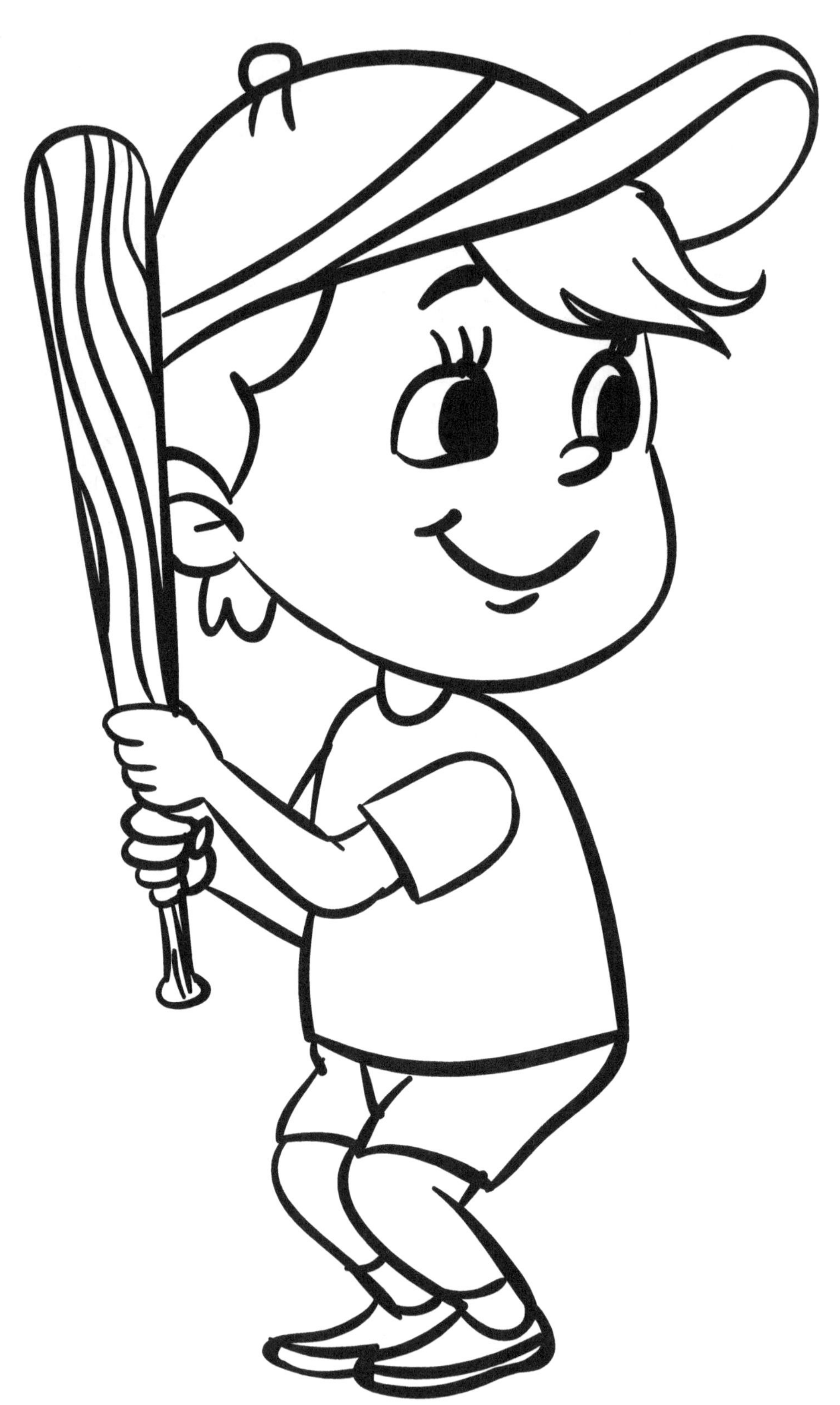

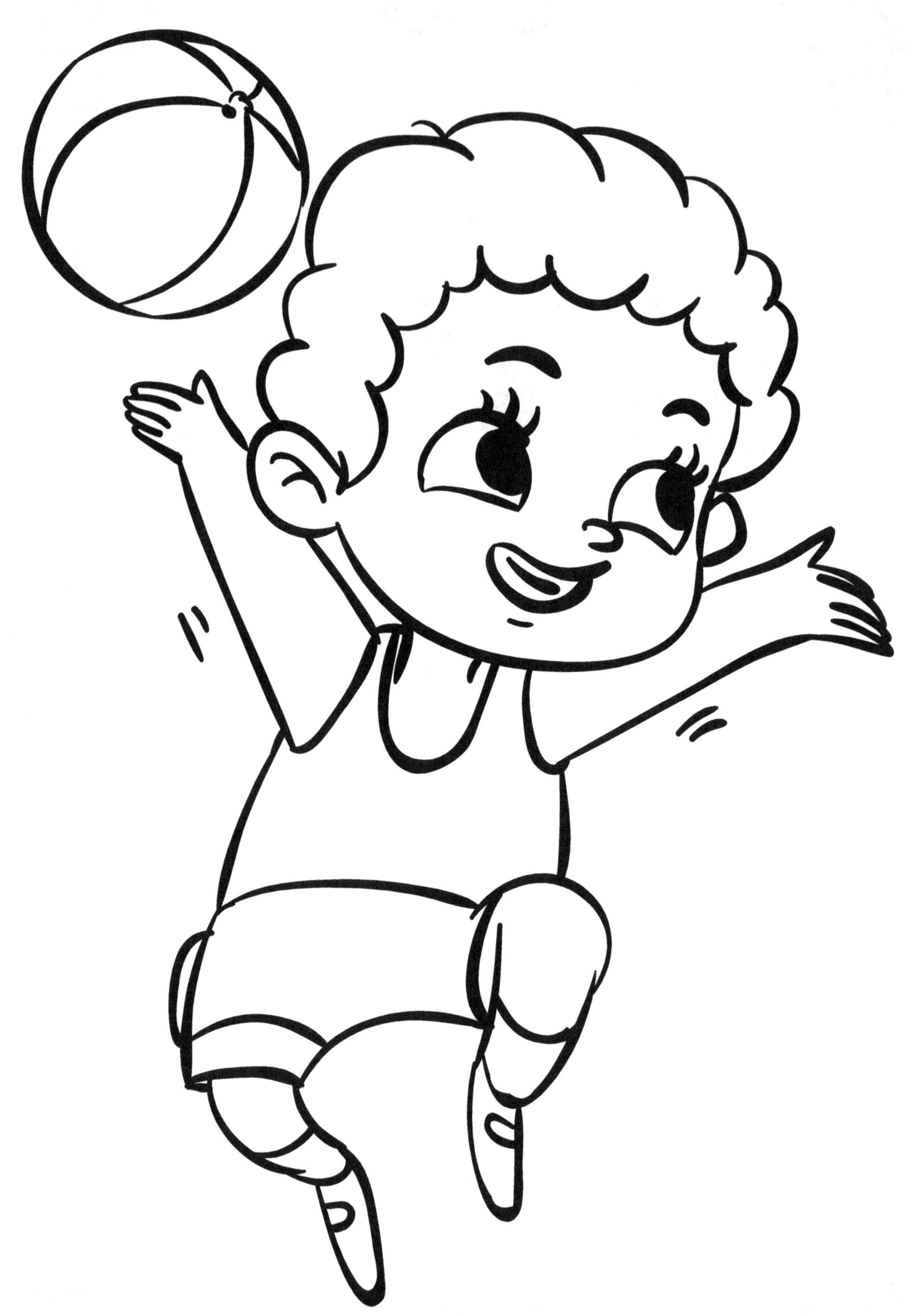

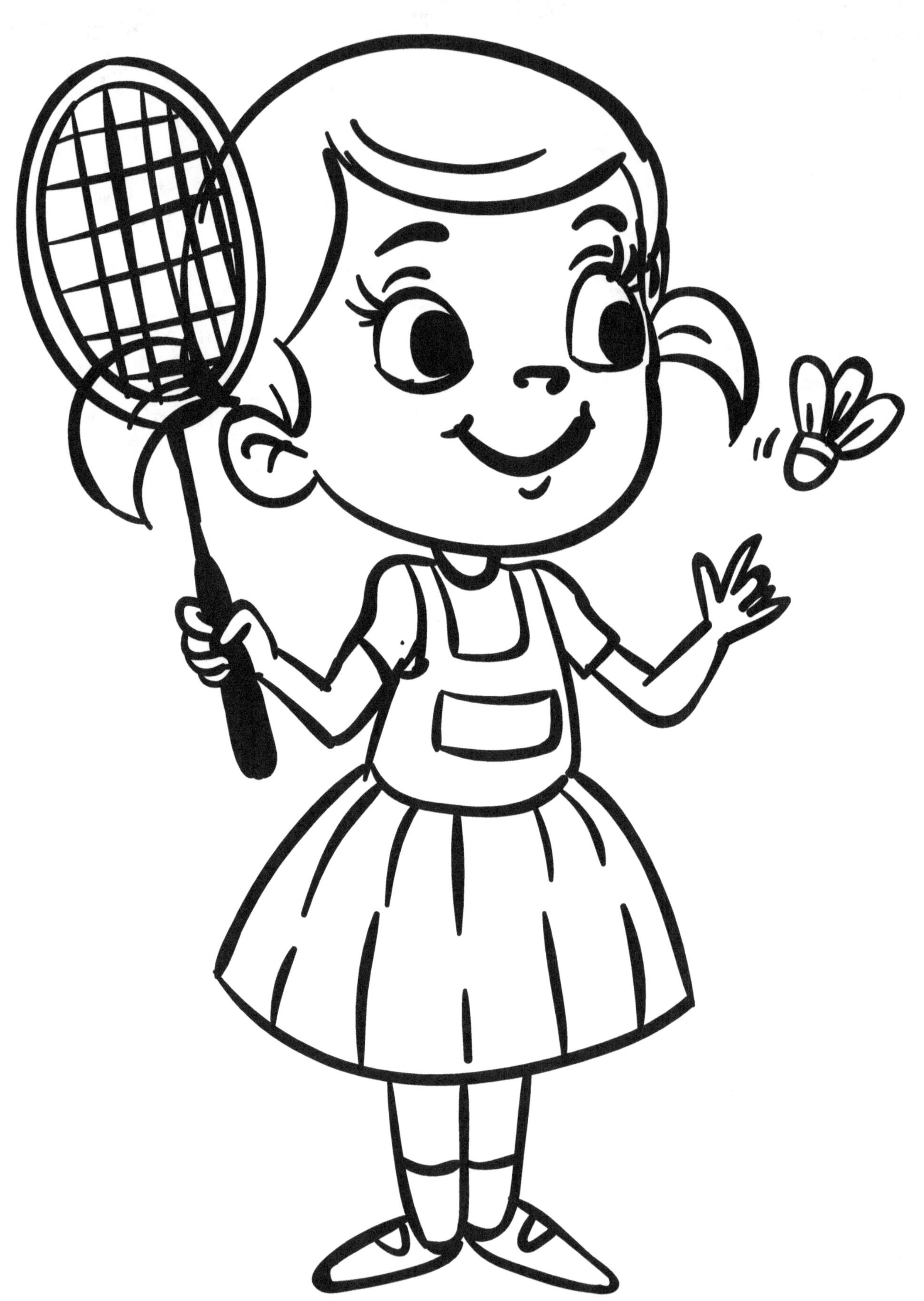

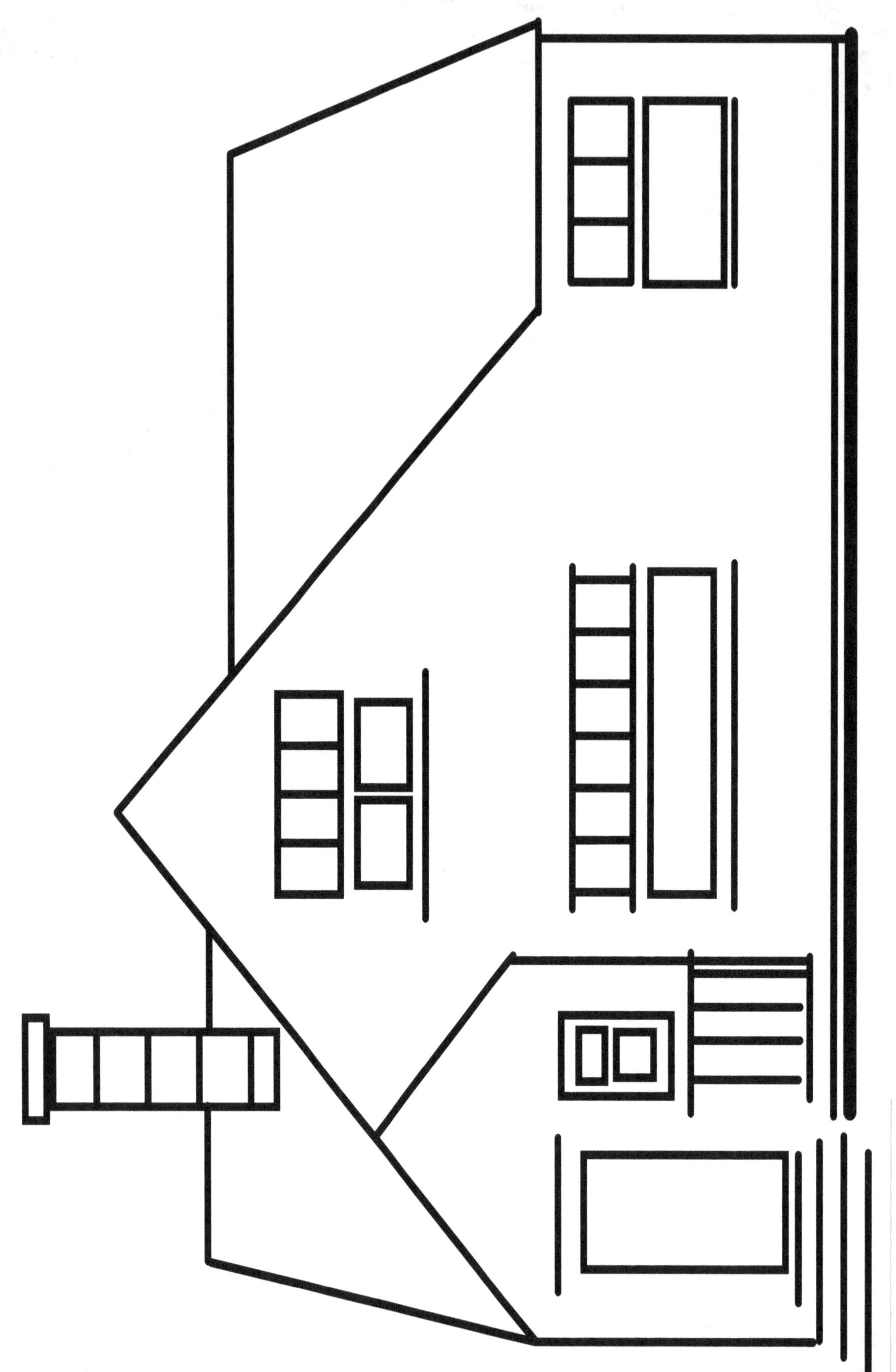

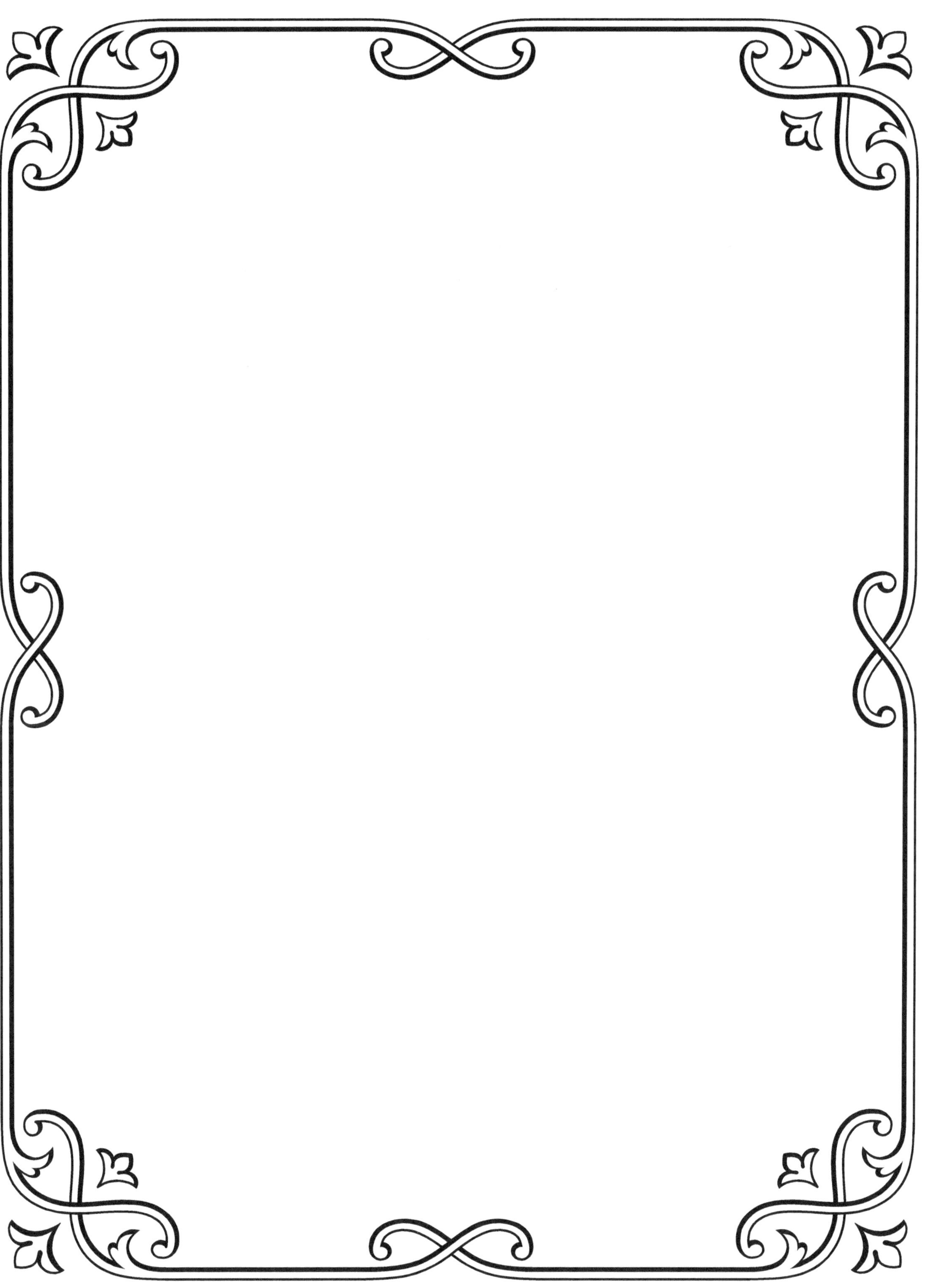

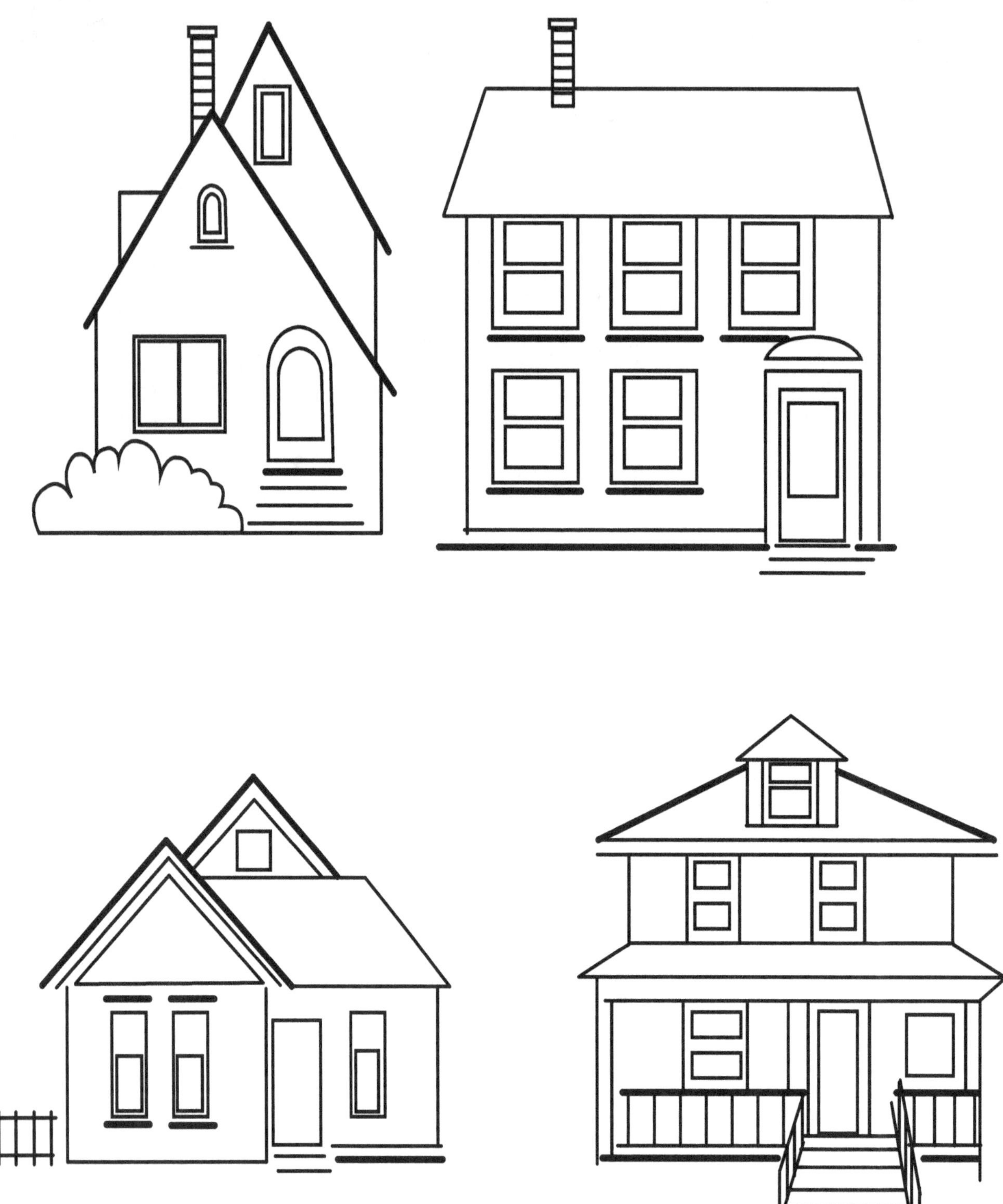

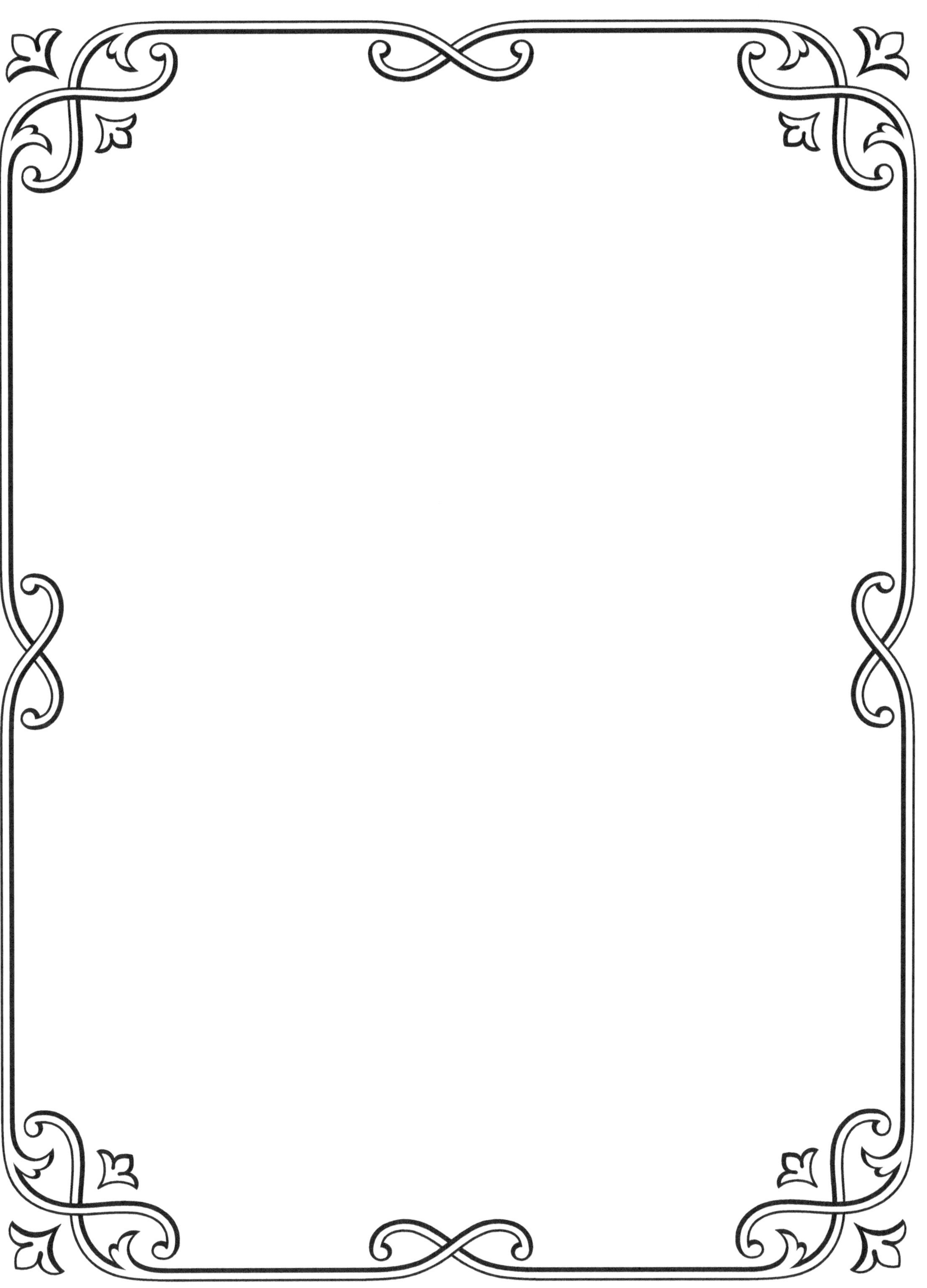